EASY TO CROCHET

EASY TO CROCHET

by Jasmin Suter

SERIES CONSULTANT: EVE HARLOW

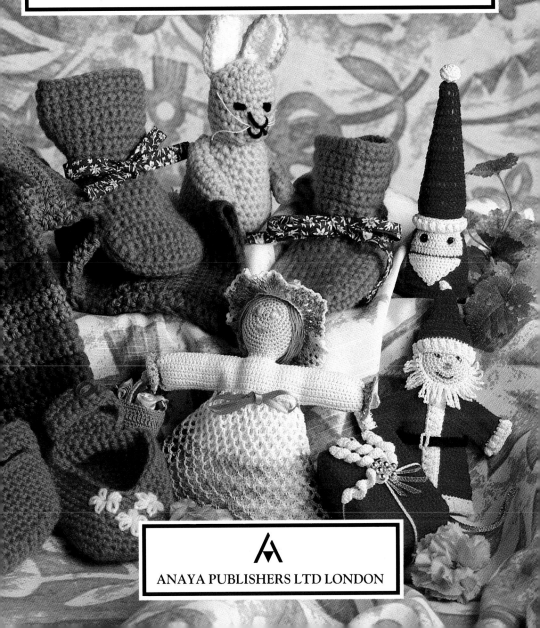

ANAYA PUBLISHERS LTD LONDON

First published in Great Britain in 1990
by Anaya Publishers Ltd, Strode House
44–50 Osnaburgh Street, London NW1 3ND
Reprinted 1991

Editor Eve Harlow
Designer Mike Leaman
Photographer Di Lewis
Illustrator Kate Simunek
Makes originator Jasmin Suter

British Library Cataloguing in Publication Data
Suter, Jasmin
Easy to crochet. — (Easy to make)
1. Crocheting
I. Title   II. Series
746.434

ISBN 1-85470-071-5

Typeset by Tradespools Limited, Frome, Somerset, UK

Printed and bound in Hong Kong
Produced by Mandarin Offset

CONTENTS

Introduction

Before starting a project, read these pages to make sure you are familiar with crochet terminology and using the correct hook size.

The increasing popularity of crafts of every kind points to a resurgence of interest and delight in hand-made, individual items. This selection of original and pretty ideas in crochet is designed with a fresh look at the craft. If you are an expert, your enthusiasm for crochet will be revived. Beginners will feel encouraged to try these simple patterns. The feeling of satisfaction and achievement experienced when making gifts for friends and family, or accessories for the home, is very special and crochet is particularly satisfying in this respect. Hand-made crochet is expensive to buy yet all you need to practise the craft is a crochet hook and yarn or thread.

Many of the projects in this book are very simply and quickly made and ideal for bazaars or fund-raising events. Most require only small quantities of yarn or thread and you may already have these left over from other crochet projects. Other items, such as the beautiful table cloth on page 34 and the baby shawl on page 12, may well become family heirlooms and be treasured for years to come.

Materials and equipment
In these pages, you'll find references to branded threads and yarns. Substitution of threads is possible, if your local needlework supplier is unable to supply the specified brand but always buy a single ball or skein first and test the tension. Perhaps you'll need a finer – or thicker – thread. You might also want to experiment with some of the patterns trying out different types of yarn with larger or smaller crochet hooks. The fascinating world of crochet is full of surprises and you may find yourself creating a beautiful piece of work, by happy chance.

Stitches
All the well-known crochet stitches are used in this book, together with special techniques like Irish and filet crochet. However, American readers will find a slight variation of terminology – see the chart on the opposite page – where European and comparative American terms are given. In the patterns only English abbreviations are given.

Hooks
In the past few years, hooks have been manufactured to international sizings. If you are using hooks you have had for some time check the size against the chart on this page. Similarly, American readers will find their hook sizes differ from the international sizings and should check the chart on the opposite page before starting a project.

Tension
Even quite experienced needlewomen sometimes spoil a piece of crochet and it is almost always the tension that is at fault. Everyone's working tension varies, particularly when working with a new type of thread, so it is recommended that you check your tension with a worked stitch sample before starting a project. The correct tension is given in every pattern where it is essential to the success of the design. If your sample matches the tension you can go ahead with the project. If the piece works larger, try a smaller hook; if the crochet is working too small, then try a larger hook until you get it exactly right.

GENERAL ABBREVIATIONS

alt	– alternate	**rep**	– repeat	**gr**	– group	**ws**	– wrong side
beg	– beginning	**rs**	– right side	**inc**	– increase	**cm**	– centimetres
ch	– chain	**rnd**	– round	**lps(s)**	– loop(s)	**mm**	– millimetres
cont	– continue	**sl**	– slip	**patt**	– pattern	**in(s)**	– inch(es)
dec	– decrease	**sp(s)**	– space(s)	**rem**	– remaining	**g**	– gram
foll	– following	**st(s)**	– stitch(es)				

HOOK SIZES

International

7.00   6.00   5.50   5.00   4.50   4.00   3.50   3.00   2.50   2.00   1.75   1.50

English

2   4   5   6   7   8   9   11   12   14   15   16

American

K/10½   J/10   I/9   H/8   G/6   F/5   E/4   D/3   C/2   B/1   5 steel   7 steel

EQUIVALENT ENGLISH AND AMERICAN TERMS

English		American	
Double crochet	(dc)	Single crochet	(sc)
Half treble	(htr)	Half double crochet	(hdc)
Treble	(tr)	Double crochet	(dc)
Double treble	(dtr)	Treble or triple crochet	(tr)
Triple treble	(ttr)	Double treble	(dtr)
Wool or yarn round hook	(wrh or yrh)	Yarn over hook	(yo)

Note: Both imperial and metric measurements are given in patterns. Work to one or the other.

1: BABIES AND CHILDREN

Pretty feet

Enchanting soft shoes to make for a special baby. Choose the blue style with fabric soles for a boy or the flower-embroidered for a girl. They are simple and quite quick to make.

BLUE SHOES

Materials
1 ball (50g) Sirdar Country Style DK; 4mm crochet hook; soft, washable cotton fabric 12in (30cm) square.
To fit
A six-month-old baby.
Tension
17 dc and 21 rows to 4in(10cm).

Upper
Make 27 ch.
1st row: 1 dc in 2nd ch from hook, 1 dc in each ch to end, turn.
2nd row: 1 ch, 1 dc in each ch to end. Rep 2nd row until work measures 2¹/₂in (6.5cm). Fasten off. Leg completed. Rejoin yarn to the 9th dc, 1 ch, 1 dc in each of next 8 dc, turn.

10

Next row: 1 ch, 2 dc in each of next 8 dc, turn. Rep last row until work measures 4¾in (12cm) from ch edge – instep completed. Fasten off.
Rejoin yarn to 1st dc on leg, 1 ch, 1 dc in each of next 8 dc, 11 dc evenly along side of instep, 1 dc in each of 9 instep sts, 11 dc evenly along other side of instep, then 1 dc in each of next 9 dc along leg.
Nest tow: 1 ch, 1 dc in each dc to end, turn. Rep last row 4 times. fasten off.

Sole
Make 7 ch for sole.
1st row: 1 ch, 1 dc in each ch to end, turn.
2nd row: 1 ch, 21 dc in next dc, 1 dc in each dc until 1 dc and ch rem, 2 dc in nest dc, 1 dc in 1 ch, turn.
3rd row: 1 ch, 1 dc in each dc to end, turn. rep last row until sole measures 4in (10cm).
Next row: 1 ch, miss 1 dc, 1 dc in each dc until 12 dc rem, miss 1 dc, 1 dc in last dc. Fasten off.

Finishing
Join leg seam. Using sole as a guide cut out 2 pieces from material. Sew crochet sole into position, then sew material sole over crochet using small slip stitches. Cut 2 fabric strips 12 × 1½in (30 × 3.7cm) for ties. Fold long edges to centre, press, fold again, stitch, neatening ends. Sew middle of ties to backs of shoes.

PINK SHOES

Materials
1 ball (50g) Sirdar Country Style DK; small amounts of contrast yarn for embroidery; 2 buttons; 4mm crochet hook.
To fit
A six-month-old baby.
Tension
10 dc and 11 rows to 2in(5cm).

Sole
Make 8 ch.
1st row: 1 dc into 2nd ch from hook, 1 dc into each ch to end, turn.
2nd row: 1 ch, 2 dc into next dc, 1 dc into each dc to last dc, 2 dc into last dc, turn.
3rd row: 1 ch, 1 dc into each dc to end, turn.

Rep 3rd row until work measures 3½in(9cm) from beg.
Next row: 1 ch, miss 1 dc, 1 dc in each dc to last 2 dc, miss 1 dc, 1 dc in last dc. Fasten off. This completes the sole.

Upper
1st round: 1 ch, 1 dc into next 7 dc, work 16 dc along side of sole, 7 dc along toe edge, then work 16 dc along other side of sole, sl st into 1 ch – 46 dc.
2nd to 4th rows: 1 ch, 1 dc into each dc to end, sl st into 1 ch.
5th round: 1 ch, 1 dc into each of next 22 dc, miss 1 dc, 1 dc into each of next 7 dc, miss 1 dc, 1 dc into each of next 15 dc, sl st into 1 ch.
6th round: 1 ch, 1 dc into each of next 22 dc, miss 1 dc, 1 dc into each of next 5 dc, miss 1 dc, 1 dc into each of next 15 dc, sl st into 1 ch.
7th round: 1 ch, 1 dc into each of next 22 dc, miss 1 dc, 1 dc into each of next 3 dc, miss 1 dc, 1 dc into each of next 15 dc, sl st into 1 ch.
8th round: 1 ch, 1 dc into each of next 22 dc, miss 1 dc, 1 dc into next dc, miss 1 dc, 1 dc into each of next 15 dc to end, sl st into 1 ch.
9th round: 1 ch, 1 dc into each of next 18 dc (miss 1 dc, 1 dc into next dc) 5 times, 1 dc into each dc to end, sl st into 1 ch. Fasten off.

Straps
Make 8 ch, 1 dc into each of 7 dc at back of heel, 9 ch, turn.
1st row: 1 dc into 2nd ch from hook, 1 dc into each of next 7 ch, 1 dc into each of next 7 dc, 1 dc into each ch to end, turn.
2nd row: 1 ch, 1 dc into next dc, 2 ch, miss 1 dc, 1 dc into each dc to end, turn.
3rd row: 1 ch, 1 dc into each dc and 1 dc into 2-ch sp, 1 dc into last dc. Fasten off.
Make a second shoe in the same way.

Finishing
Sew on buttons. Embroider three lazy daisy flowers on fronts of shoes. Alternatively, sew on a pompon or a fancy button – such as an animal or bird shape.

Sweet dreams

A simple shawl in an easy pattern which even a beginner will enjoy making. First, a centre square is worked, then the border strips are sewn around the edges. It makes a delightful gift for a new baby.

Materials
4 balls (100g) Twilleys Lyscordet or Galaxia 5; 4mm crochet hook; 6 $^5/_8$yd(6m) of $^1/_4$in(6mm)-wide Offray double faced satin ribbon.

Measurements
52in(132cm) square.

Tension
11 dc to 2in(5cm).

Centre
Make 261 ch.

1st row: 1 dc in 9th ch from hook, *5 ch, miss 3 ch, 1 dc in next ch; rep from * to end, turn.

2nd row: 7 ch, 1 dc in 3rd of next 5-ch lp, *5 ch, 1 dc in 3rd of next 5-ch lp; rep from * to end, turn.

Rep 2nd row until work measures approximately 48in(122cm) or makes a complete square. Fasten off.

Border
Make 37 ch.

1st row: 1 dc in 9th ch from hook, *5 ch, miss 3 ch, 1 dc in next ch; rep from * to end, turn.

2nd row: 7 ch to stand for 1st lp, (1 dc in 3rd of 5-ch lp, 5 tr for shell in next dc) twice, 1 dc in 3rd of 5-ch lp, 5 ch, 1 dc in 3rd of 5-ch lp, 5 ch, (1 dc in 3rd of 5-ch lp, 5 tr for shell in next dc) twice, 1 dc in 3rd of 5-ch lp, 5 ch, 1 dc in 4th ch of 7-ch lp, turn.

3rd row: 7 ch, 1 dc in 3rd of 5-ch lp, (5 ch, 1 dc in 3rd tr of next shell) twice, (5 ch, 1 dc in 3rd ch of next 5-ch lp) twice, (5 ch, 1 dc in 3rd tr of next shell) twice, 5 ch, 1 dc in 3rd ch of last lp, turn.

4th row: As 2nd row, working shells and lps in line.

Rep 3rd and 4th rows until border strip fits along one side of centre piece, work another 8in(20cm). Fasten off.

Work three more border strips in the same way.

Finishing
Sew borders to sides of centre piece gathering the fullness at corners. Sew short ends of borders together. Cut ribbon into four lengths. Thread ribbon through last but one row of loops round the centre square. Tie ends into bows at corners (see detail below).

Work the shawl in a coloured yarn for a 'cuddle-up' for a 2-3 year-old – they love bright colours at this age. Substitute plaited yarn for the ribbons.

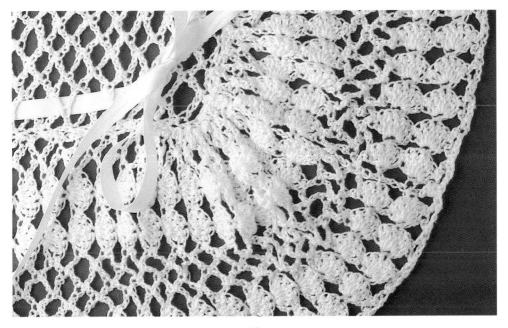

13

Baby love

Two cheerful bibs (or feeders) to make mealtimes much more fun. They are easily washed and will drip-dry quickly. Choose either the smiling cat design or the chickens; they're both worked from simple charts. Each square represents 1 dc.

HAPPY CAT

Materials
1 ball Robin Diamante in main colour (M); 1 ball in contrast colour (B), black yarn scraps; Broderie Anglaise trimming; 3.5mm crochet hook.
Measurements
6¹/₂in(16.5cm) wide.
Tension
18 dc and 24 rows to 4in(10cm).

Bib
Using M, 21 ch.
1st row: 1 dc into 2nd ch from hook, 1 dc into each ch to end, turn – 20 dc.
2nd row: 3 ch 1 dc into 2nd ch from hook, 1 dc into next ch, 1 dc into each dc to end, turn – 22 dc.
3rd row: As 2nd row – 24 dc.
Working in dc throughout, follow chart, increasing and decreasing and changing colours where indicated.

Ties
Using M, make 2 chains each 12in(30cm) long.

Cat chart

Chickens chart

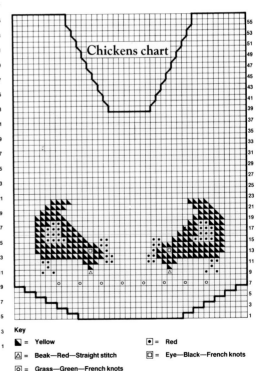

Key   ● = Blue   ◇ = White   - - - = Black-Straight stitches

Key
◼ = Yellow   ●□ = Red
△ = Beak—Red—Straight stitch   □ = Eye—Black—French knots
○ = Grass—Green—French knots

Finishing
Stitch ties at corners of bib.
Embroider features, sew on trimming.

FEEDING CHICKENS

Materials
1 ball (25g) Twilleys Lyscordet in white,
small ball in red, yellow, short length of
black; 2.5mm crochet hook.
Measurements
7in(18cm) wide.
Tension
25 dc to 4in(10cm).

Bib
Make 20 ch.
1st row: 1 dc in 2nd ch from hook, 2 dc in
each ch to end, turn.
2nd row: 3 ch, 1 dc in 2nd ch from
hook, 1 dc in next ch, 1 dc in each dc

to end, turn - 22 dc.
3rd row: As 2nd row – 24 dc.
Working in dc throughout, follow chart,
increasing and decreasing and changing
colours where indicated.

Edging
Work evenly around bib in dc having a
multiple of 3 sts, sl st to beg.
Next round: 1 ch, 1 dc in next dc, *3 ch, sl st
in last dc worked, 1 dc in each of next 3 dc;
rep from * ending 1 dc, sl st to 1 ch. Fasten off.

Ties
Make 2 chains each 12in(30cm) long.

Finishing
Sew ties to corners of bib. Work embroidery
as shown on chart with red beaks in straight
stitch and black eyes and green grass in
French knots.

Fun and games

Fun and games

Make these as single toys to hang in baby's pram or cot or sew them all along a ribbon to make a toy which will amuse baby for hours.

Materials

Cat Small ball of DK yarn in pink (A); few yards(metres) of same yarn in deep pink (B); short length of same yarn in blue (C).
Chick Small ball of DK yarn in yellow (A); few yards(metres) in blue (B); a few inches(cms) in red (C).

Rabbit Small ball of DK yarn in blue (A); a few yards(metres) in yellow (B); short lengths of dark blue (C) and red (D).
For all: 3mm crochet hook; washable polyester toy filling.
Measurements
4in(10cm) from base of body to top of head.

CAT

Body
Using A, make 4 ch, sl st to beg.
1st round: 2 ch, 5 htr in ring, sl st to beg.
2nd round: 2 ch, 1 htr in base of 2-ch,
2 htr in each of 5 htr, sl st to beg.
3rd round: 2 ch, (2 htr in next htr,
1 htr in next htr) 5 times, 2 htr in last htr, sl
st to beg.
4th round: 2 ch, (2 htr in next htr,
1 htr in each of next 2 htr) 5 times, 2 htr in
next htr, 1 htr in last htr, sl st to beg.
Fasten off.
Make another piece in the same way, but do
not fasten off.
5th round: Place 1st piece behind 2nd piece
and, lightly stuffing as you go, work 1 ch,
then working through top lp only on each
side 1 dc in each htr to end. Fasten off.

Head
Work 1st piece as given for Body for 2
rounds. Fasten off.
Work another piece but do not fasten off.
3rd round: Work as 5th rnd on Body, at the
same time sl st the last 3 dc to body.

Ears
Leaving 2 dc at top of head free rejoin A and
work 4 ch, 3 dtr in dc at one side leaving last
lp of each on hook, yrh and draw through all
lps and fasten off. Work other ear in the
same way.

Neck tie
Using B, make 16 ch, then 1 dc in 2nd ch
from hook, 1 dc in each ch to end. Fasten
off. Sew round neck.

Hanging loop
Using A, make a ch cord 3½in(9cm) long.
Sew each end to back of head.

Arms (make 2)
Using A, make 12 ch, then 1 htr in 3rd ch
from hook, 1 htr in next ch, 1 sl st to next
ch and fasten off. Sew ch end to body, as shown.

Finishing
Using B, embroider nose and mouth. Using
C embroider straight stitches for eyes.

CHICK

Using A, make **Body, Head and Hanging
loop** as given for **Cat** .

Beak
Using C, make 2 ch, 1 htr in 1st ch.
Fasten off. Sew into position.

Ears
Using A, leaving 2 dc free at top of head,
rejoin yarn and work 2 dc in dc at one side.
Fasten off. Work other ear in same way.

Feet
Using A, leaving 2 dc free in centre, rejoin
yarn and work 1 ch, 2 tr and 1 dc in dc at
one side. Fasten off. Work other foot.

Scarf
Using B, work as for **Neck tie** on **Cat**.
Place round chick, sl st one end into
position leaving other end free.

Finishing
Using B, embroider a straight stitch for each
eye.

RABBIT
Using A, make **Body, Head and Hanging
loop** as given for **Cat** .

Ears
Using A, leaving 1 dc at top of head free,
rejoin yarn and in dc at one side work 3 ch,
4 tr, turn, 3 ch, leaving last lp of each on
hook 1 tr in each of 4 tr, yrh and draw
through all lps. Fasten off.
Work other ear in the same way.

Bow
Using B, work as for **Neck tie** on **Cat** . Place
round neck and catch in position, turn ends
back to form a bow tie.

Finishing
Using A, make a small pompon and sew to
back of body for tail.

Using D, embroider nose and mouth. Using
C, embroider 2 small straight stitches for
eyes (see picture).

One, two, three

These delightful easy-to-hold grab toys will be favourites with babies, as they are soft and colourful and help them to learn about using their hands. Use the basic shapes to invent other creatures.

DUCK

Materials
1 ball (50g) Robin Columbine DK each in yellow (A) and peach (B); small amount of black; 3.5mm crochet hook; washable polyester toy filling.
Measurements
4³/₄in(12cm) long.
Tension
20 dc to 4in(10cm).

Body
With A, make 2 ch.
1st round: Work 6 dc in 2nd ch from hook, sl st to beg.
2nd round: (2 dc in each dc) to end. 12 sts.
3rd round: (2 dc in next dc, 1 dc in next dc) 6 times. 18 dc.
Cont in this way, working one more dc after inc on each rnd until there are 30 dc. Work 12 rnds straight, using safety pin to mark rnd ends and moving it up on every rnd.
Next round: (Dec over 2 dc, 1 dc in each of next 3 dc) 6 times.
Next round: (Dec over 2 dc, 1 dc in each of next 2 dc) 6 times.
Cont in this way until 6 dc remain. Stuff body then cut yarn and run end through rem 6 sts, draw up and secure.

Head
Using A, work as body to end of 2nd rnd – 12 dc. Work 3 rows straight in dc. Dec 6 sts in next rnd. Stuff head and fasten off yarn, drawing end through rem sts to close and secure. Sew head to body.

Upper beak
Using B, make 2 ch, 4 dc in 2nd ch from hook, turn, 1 ch, 1 dc in each dc. Fasten off.

Lower beak
Using B, as upper beak but after turn, 1 ch, 1 dc in 1st dc, 1 htr in centre 2 dc, 1 dc in last dc. Fasten off.
Join side edges of beak and sew to head.

Feet (make 2)
Using B, make 4 ch, 3 tr in 4th ch from hook. Fasten off. Sew to each side of body.

Finishing
With short length of black yarn, work a large French knot either side of beak for the eyes. With B, work an outline in back stitch for the wings then work a few loops at the back for the tail.

MOUSE

Materials
1 ball (50g) Robin Columbine DK each in white (A) and pink (B); small amount of black; white cotton thread; 3.5mm crochet hook; washable polyester toy filling.
Measurements
4³/₄in(12cm) long.
Tension
20 dc to 4in(10cm).

Body
Using A, make 2 ch.
1st round: 6 dc in 2nd ch from hook, sl st to beg.
2nd round: 2 dc in each dc to end – 12 sts.
3rd round: (2 dc in next st, 1 dc in next st) 6 times.
4th round: (2 dc in next st, 1 dc in each of next 2 sts) 6 times – 24 sts.
Cont straight in dc on 24 sts for 10 rnds – mark beg of each round with a safety pin, replacing it at end of each round.

Next round: (Dec over next 2 dc, 1 dc in each of next 2 dc) 6 times – 18 sts.
Work 2 rnds straight.
Next round: (Dec over 2 dc, 1 dc in next dc) 6 times.
Work 2 rnds straight.
Next round: (Dec over 2 dc) 6 times – 6 sts.
Cut yarn, run end through rem 6 sts and, after stuffing, draw up and secure to a point.

Ears (make 2)
Using A, make 2 ch. In 2nd ch from hook work 5 dc, turn, 1 dc in each of 2 dc, 3 htr in centre dc, 1 dc in each of rem dc. Fasten off.

Using B, make 2 ch, 4 dc in 2nd ch from hook, turn, 1 ch, 2 dc in 1st dc, 1 dc in each of next 2 dc, 2 dc in last dc. Fasten off.

Tail
Using B, make 19 ch. In 2nd ch from hook work 1 dc, 1 dc in each rem ch to end. Fasten off.

Finishing
Sew on tail. Sew pink ears to white and sew to head with pink to front. With black yarn work French knots for eyes. With white cotton sew whiskers.

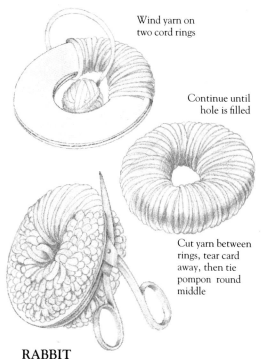

Wind yarn on two cord rings

Continue until hole is filled

Cut yarn between rings, tear card away, then tie pompon round middle

RABBIT

Materials
1 ball (50g) Robin Columbine crepe DK in blue; small amounts of white and black; 3.5mm crochet hook; washable polyester toy filling.

Measurements
4³/₄in(12cm) high.

Tension
20 dc to 4in(10cm).

Body
Make 2 ch.

1st round: 6 dc in 2nd ch from hook, sl st to 1st dc on this and foll rnds.

2nd round: (2 dc in each dc) 6 times – 12 dc.

3rd round: (2 dc in next dc, 1 dc in next dc) 6 times – 18 dc.

4th round: (2 dc in next dc, 1 dc in each of next 2 dc) 6 times – 24 dc.

5th round: (2 dc in next dc, 1 dc in each of next 3 dc) 6 times – 30 dc.

Work 8 rnds straight in dc.

14th round: (Dec 1 dc, 1 dc in each of next 3 dc) 6 times – 24 dc.

15th, 17th and 19th rounds: Work straight.

16th round: (Dec 1 dc, 1 dc in each of next 2 dc) 6 times – 18 dc.

18th round: (Dec 1 dc, 1 dc in next dc) 6 times – 12 dc.

Fasten off. Stuff body.

Head
Work as body until there are 18 dc.
Work 3 rnds straight.

Next round: (2 dc in next dc, 1 dc in next st) twice, 1 dc in each dc to end.

Next round: (2 dc in next dc, 1 dc in next dc) 3 times, 1 dc in each dc to end.

Next round: (Dec over 2 dc, 1 dc in next st) 3 times, 1 dc in each dc to end.

Next round: (Dec over 2 dc, 1 dc in next st) twice, 1 dc in each dc to end – 18 sts.

Next round: (Dec over 2 dc) 9 times – 9 sts.

Fasten off. Stuff head and sew to body with shaped section for face.

Arms (make 2)
Make 10 ch.

1st row: 1 dc in 2nd ch from hook, 1 dc in each ch to end, turn.

2nd to 7th rows: 1 ch, 1 dc in each of 8 dc, turn.

Omit turn on 7th row, then work 5 dc evenly along row ends. Fasten off.

Join into a tube, draw up lower edge and fasten off. Sew to body.

Legs (make 2)
As **arms** and sew under body allowing small section to show as feet.

Outer ears (make 2)
Using blue, make 10 ch. Miss 1st ch, then along ch work 1 dc, 1 htr, 5 tr, 1 htr, 1 dc, 1 dc in top, then work 1 dc, 1htr, 5 tr, 1 htr, 1 dc along other side of ch. Fasten off.

Inner ears (make 2)
Using white, make 8 ch, miss 1st ch, then along ch work 1 dc, 5 htr, 1 dc, 1 dc in top and rep along other side of ch. Fasten off.

Finishing
Join ear sections together and sew to head. Make white pompon for tail (see diagrams). Work French knots for eyes, stab stitches for nose and mouth.
Sew white whiskers.

Baby ball

All babies love a ball to play with and this simple two-colour patterned one is safe for young children. You could insert a large bell or rattle while stuffing to make it even more fun for them.

Materials
Small quantities of DK yarn in each of pink (A) and blue (B); 3mm crochet hook; washable polyester toy filling.

Measurements
Approximately 14½in(37cm) circumference.

Using A, make 4 ch, sl st to beg to form a ring.
1st round: 3 ch, 11 tr in ring, sl st to beg to join.
2nd round: 3 ch, (2 tr in next tr, 1 tr in next tr) 5 times, 2 tr in next tr, sl st to beg.
Join in B, noting that when changing colour draw next colour through lp on hook and pull lp tight and carry yarn not in use across back of work.
3rd round: Using A, 3 ch, 1 tr in base of 3 ch, (using B, 1 tr in each of 2 tr, using A, 2 tr in next tr) 5 times, using B, 1 tr in each of 2 tr, sl st to 3rd of 3 ch.
4th round: Using B, 3 ch, 2 tr in next tr, (using A, 1 tr in next tr, 2 tr in next tr, using B, 1 tr in next tr, 2 tr in next tr) 5 times, using A, 1 tr in next tr, 2 tr in next tr, sl st to 3rd of 3 ch.
5th round: Using A, 3 ch, 3 tr in next tr, 1 tr in next tr, (using B, 1 tr in next tr, 3 tr in next tr, 1 tr in next tr, using A, 1 tr in next tr, 3 tr in next tr, 1 tr in next tr) 5 times, using B, 1 tr in next tr, 3 tr in next tr, 1 tr in next tr, sl st to 3rd of 3 ch.
6th to 13th rounds: Alternating colours, work 1 tr in each tr as set.
14th round: Using A, 3 ch, leaving last lp of each on hook 1 tr in each of next 2 tr, yrh and draw through all lps – 1 tr decreased, dec 1 tr, (using B, dec 1 tr, 1 tr in next tr, dec 1 tr, using A, dec 1 tr, 1 tr in next tr, dec 1 tr) 5 times, using B, dec 1 tr, 1 tr in next tr, dec 1 tr, sl st to 3rd of 3 ch.

15th round: Using B, 3 ch, dec 1 tr, (using A, 1 tr in next tr, dec 1 tr, using B, 1 tr in next tr, dec 1 tr) 5 times, using A, 1 tr in next tr, dec 1 tr, sl st to 3rd of 3 ch. Break off B yarn.
16th round: Using A, 3 ch, dec 1 tr all round, sl st to 3rd of 3 ch.
Stuff firmly.
17th round: 3 ch, dec 1 tr all round. Draw up last round and fasten off.

To make smaller balls use 4-ply yarn and a 2.5mm hook. Larger balls for older children can be made using chunky yarn and a 4mm hook. You can work balls in several colours, so it is an ideal way of using up scraps of yarn.

Smart pair

These charming little sweaters are easy to make and wear. Eyecatching yet simple, make them in wool mix or cotton for winter or summer.

SWEATER WITH POCKET

Materials
2(2: 3) 50g balls Sirdar Castaway DK (MC), 1(2: 2) balls 1st contrast (A), 1(2: 2) balls 2nd contrast (B); 3 buttons; 4mm crochet hook.

Measurements
To fit 18(20: 22)in(46(51: 56)cm) chest – actual measurements: 20(22: 24) in(51(56: 61)cm); length 10(11^1/$_4$: 12^3/$_4$)in (25(28.5: 32.5)cm); sleeve 7^1/$_4$(8^3/$_4$: 10^1/$_2$)in (18.25(22.5: 26.25)cm).

Tension
18 sts and 20 rows to 4in(10cm).

Note: Figures in brackets refer to larger sizes; where only one figure is given, this refers to all sizes.

Back
Using main colour (MC), make 45(49: 53) ch.

1st row: Miss 1 ch, 1 dc in each ch to end, turn.

2nd row: 1 ch, 1 dc in each dc to end, turn. Rep 2nd row throughout working in 4 row stripes of MC, contrast A and contrast B. Cont until work measures 10(11^1/$_4$:

12^3/$_4$)in(25(28.5: 32.5)cm). Fasten off.

Front
Work as for back to last row.

Last row (button lps): 1 ch, patt 30(32: 34), 2 ch, miss 2 dc, 1 dc into each of next 7 dc, 2 ch, miss 2 dc, 1 dc in each dc to end. Fasten off.

Sleeves (both alike)
Using MC, make 33(37: 41) ch. Work 2 rows as at beg of back then cont in patt as for back until work measures 7^1/$_4$(8^3/$_4$: 10^1/$_2$)in (18.5(22.5: 26.5)cm). Fasten off.

Pocket
Using MC, make 13(15: 17) ch. Work in MC in dc until work measures 3(3^1/$_4$: 4)in (7.5(8.5: 10)cm). Fasten off.

Finishing
Join 15(17: 19) dc for right shoulder seam, and 4 dc only for left shoulder seam. Sew in the sleeves. Join side and sleeve seams in one. Sew pocket in position on left front (see picture). Sew 2 buttons to back left shoulder and work loops to correspond on opposite edge. Sew button to pocket.

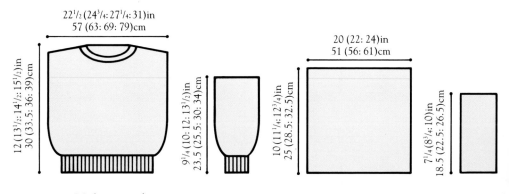

22^1/$_2$(24^3/$_4$: 27^1/$_4$: 31)in
57 (63: 69: 79)cm

12 (13^1/$_2$: 14^1/$_2$: 15^1/$_2$)in
30 (33.5: 36: 39)cm

9^1/$_4$(10: 12: 13^1/$_2$)in
23.5 (25.5: 30: 34)cm

Multi-striped sweater

20 (22: 24)in
51 (56: 61)cm

10(11^1/$_4$:12^3/$_4$)in
25 (28.5: 32.5)cm

7^1/$_4$(8^3/$_4$: 10)in
18.5 (22.5: 26.5)cm

Sweater with pocket

MULTI-STRIPED SWEATER

Materials
2(2: 3: 3) balls (50g) Sirdar Country Style DK in main colour (A); 1(1: 2: 3) balls in each of three contrast colours (B) (C) and (D); 4mm crochet hook; 2 small buttons.

Measurements
To fit 20$\frac{1}{4}$(22: 24: 26)in(51(56: 61: 66)cm) chest; actual measurement 22$\frac{1}{2}$(24$\frac{3}{4}$: 27$\frac{1}{4}$: 31) in(57(63: 69: 79)cm); length 12(13$\frac{1}{2}$: 14$\frac{1}{2}$: 15$\frac{1}{2}$)in(30(33.5: 36: 39)cm); sleeve seam 9$\frac{1}{4}$(10: 12: 13$\frac{1}{2}$)in(23.5(25.5: 30: 34)cm).

Tension
20 sts and 15 rows to 4in(10cm) measured over pattern.

Note: Figures in brackets refer to larger sizes; where only one figure is given, this refers to all sizes.

Back
With B, make 59(65: 71: 77) ch.
1st row (rs): Miss 3 ch (stands as 1 tr), 1 tr in next and each ch to end, turn – 57(63: 69: 75) sts.
2nd row: With C, 1 ch, miss 1 st, *1 tr in next st, sl st in next st; rep from * ending last rep, sl st in top of 3 ch, turn.
3rd row: With D, 3 ch (stands as 1 tr), miss 1 st, *1 tr in next tr, 1 tr in next sl st; rep from * ending last rep 1 tr in turning ch, turn.
Rep 2nd and 3rd rows for patt in colour sequence beg A, C, B, A, D, B, C, D until back measures 9$\frac{3}{4}$ (11$\frac{1}{4}$:12$\frac{1}{4}$:13$\frac{1}{4}$)in (25(29: 31:34)cm) ending after a 2nd patt row. Fasten off.
Mark centre 23(25: 27:29) sts for neck.

Front
Work as back until front is 7 rows less than back to shoulder.

Shape Neck
Next row: Patt 21(23: 25: 27) sts, turn and cont on these sts only for first side. Dec 1st at neck edge on next 4 rows. Patt 2 rows. Fasten off. 17(19: 21: 23) sts.
With rs facing, miss centre 15(17: 19: 21) sts, join yarn to next st, patt to end and complete this side to match first side, reversing shaping.

Sleeves (both alike)
With B, make 41(43: 45: 47) ch and work 3 rows as back. 39(41: 43: 45) sts.
Cont in patt inc 1st at both ends of next and every alt row to 53(55: 57: 59) sts. Cont straight until work measures 7$\frac{1}{2}$(8$\frac{1}{2}$:9$\frac{3}{4}$:11$\frac{1}{4}$)in(19(22:25:29)cm). Fasten off.

Welts
With A, make 11 ch, 1 dc in 2nd ch from hook, 1 dc in each rem ch to end, turn – 10 dc.
1st row: 1 ch, 1 dc in 1st dc, (1 dc in back loop only of next dc) to end, turn.
Rep last row until piece fits, slightly stretched, along lower edge of sweater back. Fasten off. Work second piece to correspond for front welt.

Cuffs
Work two pieces as for welts to fit cuff edge.

Finishing
Sew on welts and cuffs. Join shoulder edges leaving approximately 1$\frac{3}{4}$in(3cm) open at neck edge.
Back neck edging – join A to marked st for back neck and work 1 dc in each neck st, turn. Work 3 more rows dc. Fasten off.
Front neck edging – join A and work 1 row dc evenly around neck edge. Work 3 more rows dc, dec 4 sts evenly on 3rd of these rows. Fasten off.
Shoulder edging – Using A work 1 row dc around shoulder opening and row ends of back and front neckband rows, turn. Work second row dc working buttonhole on front edge by working 2 ch, miss 2 dc, dc to end. Fasten off.
Fold sleeves in half lengthways and, placing fold to shoulder seam, sew top edge of sleeve in place. Join side and sleeve seams. Sew on buttons.

Either of the two sweaters can be made in one colour only for a different look. Alternatively, you could work two contrasting stripes around the cuffs and welt.

2: HOME COMFORTS

Cushioned for comfort

Choose either the dainty crocheted lace cover for a feminine and pretty look or the Aran-style alternative with its chunky feeling of country traditions. Although light shades have been used here, the lacy cover could be worked in a bright pastel colour or black while the Aran style would look effective in browns or russets.

FLOWERS AND LACE

Materials
3 balls (50g) Twilleys Stalite in main colour
(M); small amounts of 2 other colours (B,
C) for flowers and leaves (optional); 3.5mm
crochet hook.
Measurements
16in(40cm) square

Tension
12 ch sps and 10 rows to 4in(10cm) when
slightly stretched.

Front
With M, make 90 ch.
Foundation row: 1 tr in 4th ch from hook,
*1 ch, miss 1 ch, 1 tr in next ch; rep from *
to end, turn – 43 ch sps.

Next row: 4 ch, miss 1st tr and ch, 1 tr in next tr, *1 ch, miss 1 ch, 1 tr in next tr, *1 ch, miss 1 ch, 1 tr in next tr; rep from * to end, working last tr in 3rd of 4 ch, turn. Rep last row 3 times.

Left side strip
Next row: 4 ch, miss 1st tr and ch, 1 tr in next tr, work 4 more ch sps, turn. Work 25 more rows on these 5-ch sps. Fasten off.
With ws facing, rejoin yarn to 5th ch sp from end and complete right side strip to match left side strip. Fasten off.

Top strip
With ws facing, rejoin yarn to 1st tr of left strip with 4 ch, miss 1st tr and ch, 1 tr in next tr, work 4 more ch sps, make 65 ch and join to right side strip by working 1 tr into 1st tr, then cont with ch sps to end, turn.
Next row: Work ch sps to within ch, cont as foundation row along ch, then cont in ch sps

to end, turn. Work 41 more rows of ch sps. Fasten off. 37 rows form cushion back.

Centre
With rs facing, rejoin yarn to last tr of right side strip row and work 1 tr in each ch sp and tr to end, sl st in 1st tr of left side strip, *turn work, miss 1st tr, sl st through next 2 tr, turn work *, cont to work up left side strip with 2 tr in each sp ending with a sl st through 2nd sp on next edge, rep from * to *, cont along top edge with 1 tr in each tr and ch sp to within last edge, rep from * to * and complete right side strip as for left side strip, ending with sl st through 3rd tr on 1st edge, turn work, sl st through next 2 tr, turn work.

Filigree
1st row: 1 ch, miss 1 tr, 1 tr in next tr, *3 ch, miss 2 tr, 1 tr in next tr; rep from * to within last tr, 1 ch, sl st through 2nd, 3rd and 4th tr of 2nd edge, turn.
2nd row: *3 ch, 1 tr in 3-ch sp; rep from * to last 3-ch sp, 3 ch, miss 2 tr from side edge, sl st in next 2 tr, turn.
3rd row: 1 ch, 1 tr in next ch sp, *3 ch, 1 tr in next ch sp; rep from * to last 3- ch sp, 1 ch, miss 2 tr from side edge, sl st in next 2 tr, turn. Rep 2nd and 3rd rows 10 times more.
Next row: 1 ch, remove hook from lp, insert hook through 2nd tr on top tr edge and pull lp through, 1 ch, 1 tr in 3-ch sp, *1 ch, miss 2 tr on top tr edge, remove hook from lp, insert hook through 3rd tr on top tr edge and pull lp through, 1 ch, 1 tr in 3-ch sp*; rep from * to * to within last tr on top tr edge, 1 ch, sl st through 2nd tr on side edge. Fasten off.

Flower motif (make 5)
With M (or C), make 5 ch, join with sl st to form a ring. **1st round:** 1 dc in ring, *3 ch, 1 dc in ring; rep from * twice, ending 3 ch, sl st in 1st dc-4 sps.
2nd round: Sl st in ch sp, work 1 dc, 5 tr, 1 dc in each ch sp to end.
3rd round: 8 ch, sl st around post of 2nd dc on 1st rnd, *8 ch, sl st around post of next dc on 1st rnd; rep from * ending last rep, 8 ch, sl st in back of dc.
4th round: Sl st in ch sp, work 1 dc, 11 tr, 1 dc in each ch sp all round, sl st in 1st dc. Fasten off.

Finishing

With right side facing, work 3 sides of cover together with pct edge, inserting hook through both layers, 1 dc, *3 ch, 1 dc in 1st of 3-ch, 1 dc in next ch sp; rep from * along three edges, working 2 pcts on each corner. Insert cushion pad, then cont pct edge along remaining side. Sew motifs in place as shown in the picture on pages 30–31.

COUNTRY STYLE

Materials

2 balls (100g) Spectrum Strata Aran yarn; 5.5mm crochet hook; 14in(35cm) zip fastener.

Measurements

16in(41cm) square

Tension

14 tr and 7 rows to 4in(10cm) measured over trs.

Special abbreviation

cl - cluster thus: 5 tr in next sp or st, remove hook, insert hook in first of 5 tr then into dropped lp, yrh and draw through all lps, 1 ch to complete.

Front

Make 4 ch and join into circle with sl st.
1st round: 3 ch stands as 1st tr, (cl in ring, 3 ch) 4 times, join to 1st cl.
2nd round: 3 ch, *cl in next 3-ch sp, 3 ch, cl in same sp, 5 ch; rep from * 3 times, join with sl st, to top of 3 ch.
3rd round: 3 ch, *cl in next 3-ch sp, 3 ch, cl in same sp, 3 ch, 3 tr in 5-ch sp, 3 ch; rep from * to end, join with sl st to top of 3 ch.
4th round: 3 ch, *cl in next 3-ch sp, 3 ch, cl in same sp, 3 ch, 1 tr in 3-ch sp, 2 ch, 1 tr in each of 3 tr, 2 ch, 1 tr in 3- ch sp, 3 ch; rep from * to end, join with sl st.
5th round: *Cl 3 ch cl all in corner sp, 3 ch, 1 tr in 3-ch sp, 2 ch, 1 tr in 2-ch sp, 2 ch, 1 tr in each of 3 tr, 2 ch, 1 tr in 2-ch sp, 2 ch, 1 tr in 3-ch sp, 3 ch; rep from * to end, join with sl st.
6th round: *Cl 3 ch cl all in corner sp, 3 ch, cl in next 3-ch sp, (2 ch, 1 tr in next tr) twice, 2 ch, 1 tr in each of 3 tr, (2 ch, 1 tr in next tr) twice, 2 ch, cl in next 3-ch sp, 3 ch; rep from * to end, join with sl st.

Stems

Use either M (or C) for stems.
1. Cut three lengths of yarn each 12½in(32cm) long, knot one end. Using the strands as a base work 50 dc over them. Fasten off. Stem length 9½in(24cm).
2. Cut three lengths of yarn each 21in(53cm) long, knot one end. Work 87 dc over strands. Fasten off. Stem length 17¾in(45cm).
3. Cut three lengths of yarn each 13½in(34cm) long and knot one end. Work 47 dc over strands. Fasten off. Stem length 10½in(27cm).

Double leaf (make 2)

With M (or C), cut three lengths of yarn, each 9¾in(25cm), knot one end.
Work along strands, *2 dc, 2 htr, 9 tr, 2 htr, 2 dc*, rep from * to *, turn, work second leaf side by rep from * to * twice. Fasten off.

7th round: Sl st along into corner 3 ch sp, *3 tr, 3 ch, 3 tr in corner sp, 3 ch, miss 1 cl, 1 dc in cl of 6th rnd, 3 ch, miss 1 tr, cl in next 2-ch sp, 2 ch, 1 tr in next 2-ch sp, 2 ch, 1 tr in each of 3 tr, 2 ch, 1 tr in next 2-ch sp, 2 ch, cl in next 2-ch sp, 2 ch, dc in top of next cl, 3 ch; rep from * to end, join with sl st to top of 3 ch.

8th round: Sl st along into corner sp, 3 ch, 2 tr 3 ch 3 tr all in same sp, *1 tr in each of 3 tr, 2 tr in next 2-ch sp, 2 ch, 1 dc in cl of 7th rnd, 2 ch, miss next tr, cl in next 2-ch sp, 5 ch, cl in next 2-ch sp, 2 ch, dc in cl of 7th rnd, 2 ch, 2 tr in next 2-ch sp, 1 tr in each of 3 tr, 3 tr, 3 ch, 3 tr in corner sp; rep from * omitting last corner sp, join with sl st to top of 3 ch.

9th round: Sl st along into corner sp, 3 ch, 2 tr, 3 ch, 3 tr into corner sp, *1 tr in each of 8 tr, 2 tr in next 2 ch sp, 2 ch, dc in cl of 8th rnd, 2 ch, cl in 5-ch sp, 2 ch, dc in cl of 8th rnd, 2 ch, 2 tr in next 2- ch sp, 2 ch, 1 tr in each of 8 tr, 3tr, 3ch, 3tr in corner sp; rep form * to end omitting last corner sp, join with sl st to top of 3 ch.

10th round: Sl st along into corner sp, 3 ch, 2 tr, 3 ch, 3 tr into corner sp, *1 tr into each of 13 tr, 2 tr in 2-ch sp, 3 ch, miss cl of 9th rnd, 2 tr in 2-ch sp, 1 tr in each of 13 tr, 3 tr, 3 ch, 3 tr in corner sp; rep from * to end, omitting last corner sp, join with sl st to top of 3 ch.

11th round: Sl st along into corner sp, 3 ch 2 tr 3 ch 3 tr into same sp, *1 tr in each tr to 3-ch sp, 1 tr 1 ch 1 tr in 3- ch sp, 1 tr in each tr to corner sp, 3 tr 3 ch 3 tr in corner sp; rep from * omitting last corner sp, join with sl st to top of 3 ch.

12th round: Sl st along into corner sp, 3 ch 2 tr 3 ch 3 tr in same sp, *1 tr in each tr to 1-ch sp, 1 ch, 1 tr in each tr to corner sp, 3 tr 3 ch 3 tr in corner sp; rep from * to end, omitting last corner sp, sl st to top of 3 ch.

13th round: Sl st along into corner sp, 3 ch 2 tr 3 ch 3 tr in same sp, *(1 tr in next tr, 2 ch, miss 2 tr) 8 times, 1 tr in next tr, 1 ch, (1 tr in next tr, 2 ch, miss 2 tr) 8 times, 1 tr in next tr, 3 tr 3ch 3tr in corner sp; rep from * omitting last corner sp, join with sl st to top of 3 ch.

14th round: Sl st along into corner sp, 3 ch, 2 tr 3 ch 3 tr in same sp, *1 tr in each of next 3 tr, (2 ch, miss 1 tr, cl in next 2-ch sp) 8 times, 2 ch, 1 tr in 1-ch sp, (2 ch, miss 1 tr, cl in next 2-ch sp) 8 times, 2ch, miss 1 tr, 1 tr in each of next 3 tr, 3 tr 3 ch 3 tr in next corner sp; rep from * to end, omitting last corner sp, join with sl st to top of 3 ch. Fasten off.

Back

Make 60 ch. 1 tr in 4th ch from hook, 1 tr in each ch to end, turn – 58 sts.

Next row: 3 ch (stands as 1st tr), miss 1 tr, 1 tr in each tr to end, turn.

Rep last row until work measures 16in(41cm). Do not fasten off. With ws of work together, work 1 row dc evenly around three sides, joining the edges, working 3 dc in each corner. Do not turn, but work dc along opening edge. Work 1 row reversed dc (dc from left to right) along the dc corner of front and around three joined edges, join with sl st and fasten off.

Finishing

Sew in zip fastener. Join remainder of seam, sewing behind the reversed dc border.

Lovely in lace

A lacy tablecloth is truly a thing of beauty, to enjoy forever. Crocheted in a simple, open stitch, you'll treasure this one for years to come.

Materials

18 balls Twilleys Twenty '20'; 1.25mm crochet hook.

Measurements

38in(97cm) square.

Tension

1 motif 2½in(6cm).

Special abbreviation

2 tr gr – 2 treble group, thus: yrh and into next sp, pull lp through, yrh and through 2 lp (2 lps on hook), yrh and into same sp, pull lp through, yrh and through 2 lp (3 lps on hook), yrh and through all lps on hook.

1st motif – 1st row

Commence with 8 ch, sl st into 1st ch to form a ring.

1st round: 3 ch (standing as 1st tr), 15 tr into ring, sl st into top of 3 ch.

2nd round: 5 ch, 1 tr into next tr, *2 ch, 1 tr into next tr; rep from * all rnd, ending last rep 2 ch, sl st into 3rd of 5 ch.

3rd round: Sl st into 1 ch and into sp, 5 ch, 1 tr into next sp, *3 ch, 1 tr into next sp; rep from * all rnd, ending last rep 3 ch,

sl st into 3rd of 5 ch.

4th round: Sl st into sp, 3 ch 4 tr 3 ch 5 tr into same sp as sl st, *miss 1 sp, 5 tr 3 ch 5 tr into next sp; rep from * all rnd, ending sl st into top of 3 ch.

5th round: Sl st into 4 tr and into sp, 3 ch 2 tr 3 ch 3 tr into same sp as sl st, *5 ch, 3 tr 3 ch 3 tr into next 3-ch sp; rep from * all rnd, finishing 5 ch, sl st into top of 3 ch.

6th round: Sl st into 2 tr, 1 dc into sp, *(5 ch 1 dc) 3 times into same sp as dc, 4 ch, miss 2 ch, 1 dc into next ch, 4 ch, 1 dc into 3-ch sp, (5ch, 1 dc) 3 times into same sp as last dc, 4 ch, miss 2 ch, 1 dc into next ch, 13 ch, sl st into top of dc just made, 4 ch, 1 dc into next 3-ch sp; rep from * all rnd, finishing last rep sl st instead of dc into 1st dc. Fasten off. This completes one motif.

2nd motif

As 1st motif to end of 5th rnd.

6th round: Sl st into 2 tr, 1 dc into sp, (5 ch 1 dc) 3 times into same sp as dc, 4 ch, miss 2 ch, 1 dc into next ch, 4 ch, 1 dc into next sp, (5 ch 1 dc) 3 times into same sp

35

as last dc, 4 ch, miss 2 ch, 1 dc into next ch, 6 ch, sl st into centre ch of 13 ch lp on 1st motif, 6 ch, sl st into dc on 2nd motif *4 ch, 1 dc 5ch 1 dc into next sp, 2 ch, sl st into centre 5 ch sp on 1st motif, 2 ch, 1 dc into same sp as last dc on 2nd motif, 5 ch, 1 dc into same sp as last dc, 4 ch, miss 2 ch, 1 dc into next ch; rep from * once, 6 ch, sl st into centre ch of 13 ch lp, on 1st motif, 6 ch, sl st into dc on 2nd motif, 4 ch, 1 dc into next sp. Cont from * to end as 6th rnd on 1st motif.

Rep 2nd motif to form row of 14 motifs.

1st motif – 2nd row
Rep 2nd motif on 1st row, working 2nd lp 6 ch, sl st into same ch, as lp on 2nd motif.

2nd motif
As 1st motif to end of 5th round.

6th round: Sl st into 2 tr, 1 dc into sp, (5 ch 1 dc) 3 times into same sp as dc, 4 ch, miss 2 ch, 1 dc into next ch, 4 ch, 1 dc into next sp, (5 ch 1 dc) 3 times into same sp as last dc, 4 ch, miss 2 ch, 1 dc into next ch, 6 ch, sl st into centre ch of 13 ch lp on previous motif, 6 ch, sl st into dc on 2nd motif *4 ch, 1 dc 5 ch 1 dc into next sp, 2 ch, sl st into centre 5 ch sp on previous motif, 2 ch, 1 dc into same sp as last dc on 2nd motif, 5 ch, 1 dc into same sp as last dc, 4 ch, miss 2 ch, 1 dc into next ch, rep from * once, 6 ch, sl st into same ch as join of previous motifs, 6 ch, sl st into dc on 2nd motif, rep from * to * twice, 6 ch, sl st into centre of 13 ch lp on previous row motif, 6 ch, sl st into dc on 2nd motif, 4 ch, 1 dc into next sp, cont to end as 1st motif. Cont as last motif until 14 motifs have been joined.

Make and join a further 12 rows of motifs.

Edging
1st round: Join into corner lp, 3 ch, 4 tr 3 ch 5 tr into same sp as join, * 4 ch, 1 dc into centre 5 ch sp, (4 ch 1 tr) into each of the next two 4-ch sps, 4 ch, 1 dc into centre 5-ch sp, (4 ch 1 tr) into each of the next 4 sps, 4 ch, 1 dc into centre 5-ch sp, (4 ch 1 tr) into each of the next 2 sps, 4 ch, 1 dc into centre 5 ch sp. Cont in this way until 4 ch, 1 dc into 5 ch sp has been worked 4 ch, 5 tr 3 ch 5 tr into corner lp; rep from * all round, finish last rep 4 ch, sl st to top of 3 ch.

2nd round: Sl st into 4 tr and into sp, 3 ch 2 tr 3 ch 3 tr 3 ch 3 tr into same sp as sl st, *(2 tr 2 ch 2 tr) into each sp to next corner, 3 tr 3 ch 3 tr 3 ch 3 tr into corner sp; rep from * all round, finish last rep sl st into top of 3 ch.

3rd round: Sl st into 2 tr and into sp, 3 ch 2 tr 3 ch 3 tr into same sp as sl st, *5 ch, 3 tr 3 ch 3 tr into next sp, (5 ch, 1 dc) into each sp to corner, 5 ch, 3 tr 3 ch 3 tr into sp; rep from * all round, finish last rep 5 ch, sl st into top of 3 ch.

4th round: Sl st into 2 tr and into sp, 3 ch, 2 tr 3 ch 3 tr into same sp as sl st, *4 ch, 1 dc into next sp, 4 ch, 3 tr 3 ch 3 tr into next sp, (5 ch 1 dc) into each sp to corner, 4 ch, 3 tr 3 ch 3 tr into next sp; rep from * all round, finish last rep 5 ch, sl st into top of 3 ch.

5th round: Sl st into 2 tr and into sp, 3 ch 2 tr 3 ch 3 tr into same sp as sl st *(4 ch, 1 dc) into each of the next 2 sps, 4 ch, 3 tr 3 ch 3 tr into next sp, (5 ch, 1 dc) into each sp to centre sp along side, 5 ch, 1 dc into same sp as last dc, (5 ch, 1 dc) into each sp to corner, 5 ch, 3 tr 3 ch 3 tr into sp; rep from * all round, finish 5 ch, sl st into top of 3 ch.

6th round: Sl st into 2 tr and into sp, 3 ch, 8 tr into same sp as sl st, *1 dc into next sp, (4 ch 1 dc into next sp) twice, 9 tr into next sp, (1 dc into next sp, 4 ch, 1 dc into next sp, 9 tr into next sp) until 2 tr rem from corner, 1 dc into sp, 4 ch, 1 dc into next sp, 9 tr into next sp; rep from * all round, finish last rep, 4 ch, 1 dc into sp, sl st into top of 3 ch.

7th round: 4 ch, 1 tr into next tr, (1 ch, 1 tr) into each of the next 7 tr, *(1 ch, 1 dc into sp) twice, (1 ch, 1 tr) into each of the next 9 tr, 1 ch, 1 dc into sp, rep from * all round finishing 1 ch, sl st into 2nd of 4 ch.

8th round: Sl st into sp, 2 ch, 1 htr into sp, (1 ch, 2 tr gr into next sp) 7 times, *1 ch, 1 dc into next dc, (1 ch, 2 tr gr into next sp) 8 times; rep from * all round finishing 1 ch, 1 dc into dc, 1 ch, sl st into top of 2 ch.

9th round: Sl st into sp, *(3 ch, 1 dc) into each 1-ch sp; rep from * all round, finish sl st into sl st. Fasten off.

Finishing
Press flat with a hot iron over a damp cloth and iron dry.

A touch of the Irish

Add charm to your party table with pretty serviette rings made of filet crochet. Finish them with a small, Irish crochet rose.

Materials
1 ball (20g) Twilley's Forty or Twenty will make 5 rings; 1mm crochet hook.
Measurements
2in(5cm) wide.
Tension
7 sps and 5 rows to 1¼in(3cm).

Ring
Make 27 ch.
1st row: 1 tr in 5th ch from hook, *1 ch, miss next ch, 1 tr in next ch; rep from * to end, turn.
2nd row: 4 ch, (stands as 1 tr, 1 ch), *1tr in next tr, 1 ch; rep from * ending 1 tr in last tr, turn. Rep 2nd row until work measures 5½in(14cm). Fasten off.

Join narrow ends. Work a row of dc evenly around edges, join with sl st and fasten off.

Rose
Make 3 ch and join with sl st to form a ring.
1st round: 16 dc in ring, join with sl st to 1st dc.
2nd round: *5 ch, miss 1 dc, dc in next dc; rep from * 6 times, 5 ch, sl st in bottom of 5 ch – 8 lps.
3rd round: (1 dc 5 tr 1 dc) in each lp.
4th round: *5 ch at back of trs, 1 dc in next dc of 2nd rnd; rep from * ending 5 ch, sl st in bottom of 5 ch.
5th round: Sl st into ch sp, (1 dc 7 tr 1 dc) in each ch sp, ending sl st in 1st dc. Fasten off. Sew rose to ring.

Curtain charm

Old-fashioned charm will grace your windows when you hold curtains back with an attractive tie. This design can be made to match your decor by threading satin or velvet ribbons through the crochet.

Materials (for 2 ties)
1–2 balls (20g) Twilleys Twenty: 1.25mm crochet hook; Offray single faced satin ribbon as required.
Measurements
1$\frac{1}{2}$in(4cm) wide.
Tension
8 sps to 2in(5cm).

Make 8 ch.
1st row: 1 tr in 8th ch from hook (sp made) * 5 ch, turn, miss 2 ch, 1 tr in next ch, rep from * for length required, having an even number of sps, ending 1 tr in 3rd of 5 ch, turn.
2nd row: * 2 dc in sp, 1 dc in next st, 2 dc in sp, 1 dc in next st, 2 ch, sl st to dc (a picot formed); rep from * until 2 sps rem, ending 2 dc in sp, 1 dc in next st, 2 dc in sp, turn.
3rd row: 3 ch, miss 1 dc, leaving last lp of each on hook work 2 dtr in next dc, yrh and draw through all lps on hook (dtr group formed), * miss (2 dc 1 picot 2 dc), 3 dtr gr in next dc, (4 ch, 2 dtr gr in 4th ch from hook) twice, 3 dtr gr in same place as last dtr gr; rep from * ending miss (2 dc 1 pct 2 dc), 3 dtr gr in next dc, 4 ch, 2 dtr gr in 4th ch from hook, turn.
4th row: 1 dc in top of dtr gr, * 5 ch, 1 dc between next two dtr grs; rep from * ending 5 ch, work a 3 dtr gr in same st as join of 3 dtr grs – thus forming a fourth gr, turn.
5th row: 1 dc in top of dtr gr, * 3 dc, 2 ch, sl st in last dc (a picot formed), 2 dc in 5-ch sp, 1 dc in dc; rep from * to end, working 1 dc in top of dtr gr on last rep, turn.
6th row: 5 ch, 1 tr in next dc, * 2 ch, miss (1 dc 1 picot 1 dc), 1 tr in next dc, 2 ch, miss 2 dc, 1 tr in next dc; rep form * ending

2 ch, miss (1 dc 1 picot 1 dc), 1 tr in next dc, 2 ch, 1 tr in last dc, turn.
Note There will be an odd number of sps.
1st round: * 2 dc in each sp across until 1 sp remains, 5 dc in next sp, 1 dc in each row end and 2 dc in dtrs across side edge, 5 dc in corner sp; rep from * all round, ending 3 dc in 1st sp, sl st to 1st dc.
2nd round: 2 dc, 1 picot all rnd. Fasten off.

Finishing
Thread $\frac{1}{4}$in(6mm)-wide ribbon through the tie's edging if desired. To suspend the tie, sew covered brass curtain rings to both ends. These slip over a hook or fixture on the wall. To cover brass rings, work buttonhole stitch all round, using matching thread.

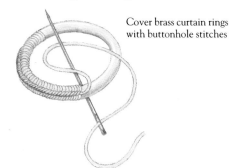

Cover brass curtain rings with buttonhole stitches

Sew rings to ends of curtain ties

38

Kitchen capers

Pot luck

Three cheerful pot holders to brighten up the kitchen, they're practical and very easy to make. Just the thing for using up yarn oddments.

CHEQUER

Materials
1 ball (50g) Robin Columbine DK in each of 2 colours; 3mm crochet hook.
Measurements
6³/₄in(17.5cm) square.
Tension
20 dc and 24 rows to 4in(10cm).

1st Strip (work 2)
Using 1st colour, make 12 ch.
1st row: 1 dc into 2nd ch from hook, 1 dc into each ch to end – 11 dc.
2nd row: 1 ch, 1 dc into each dc to end.
Rep 2nd row throughout.
Work 11 more rows in 1st colour, 13 rows in 2nd colour and 13 rows in 1st colour.
Fasten off.

2nd Strip
Work as given for 1st strip using 2nd colour for 13 rows, 1st colour for 3 rows, 2nd colour for 2 rows, 1st colour for 3 rows, 2nd colour for 2 rows, 1st colour for 3 rows and 2nd colour for 13 rows. Fasten off.
Join the three strips together.
Using 2nd colour, work 1 row of dc around the four edges.
Next round: *3 ch, miss 1 dc, 1 dc into next dc; rep from * ending 3 ch, sl st into 1st ch, 15 ch, sl st into previous sl st. Fasten off.
Make and attach hanger ch.

STAR

Materials
1 ball (50g) Robin Columbine DK in each of 4 colours; 3mm crochet hook.
Measurements
7¹/₄in(18.5cm) in diameter.
Tension
18 tr and 10 rows to 4in(10cm).

Special abbreviation
Crab st thus – Work as dc but work from left to right.

Using 1st colour make 3 ch and sl st in 1st ch to form a ring.
1st round: 1 ch, 16 dc into ring, sl st in 1 ch.
2nd round: 3 ch, 1 tr into next dc, (2 ch, miss 1 dc, 2 tr into next dc) 7 times 2 ch, sl st into 3rd ch.
3rd round: Sl st into next tr and 2-ch sp, 3 ch 1 tr 2 ch 2 tr into same sp, (2 tr 2 ch 2 tr into next sp) 7 times sl st into 3rd ch.
4th round: Sl st into next tr and 2-ch sp. Using 2nd colour 3 ch 2 tr 2 ch 3 tr into same sp, (3 tr 2 ch 3 tr into next sp) 7 times, sl st into 3rd ch.
5th round: Sl st into next 2 tr and 2-ch sp. Using 3rd colour, 3 ch 2 tr 3 ch 3 tr into same sp, (3 tr 2 ch 3 tr into next sp) 7 times, sl st into 3rd ch.
6th round: Sl st into next 2 tr and 3-ch sp. Using 4th colour 3 ch 3 tr 3 ch 4 tr into same sp, 1 ch, (4 tr 3 ch 4 tr into next sp, 1 ch) 7 times, sl st into 3rd ch.
7th round: Using 1st colour 1 ch, 1 dc into next 3 tr, 4 dc into sp, 1 dc into next 4 tr, 1 dc into 1 ch sp, (1 dc into next 4 tr, 4 dc into sp, 1 dc into next 4 tr, 1 dc into 1-ch sp) 7 times, sl st into 1 ch.
8th round: 1 ch, 1 dc into next 4 dc, 2 dc into next 2 dc, (1 dc into next 11 dc, 2 dc into next 2 dc) 7 times, 1 dc into next 6 dc, sl st into 1 ch.
9th round: Using 2nd colour 1 ch, 1 dc into next 5 dc, 2 dc into next 2 dc, (1 dc into next 13 dc, 2 dc into next 2 dc) 7 times, 1 dc into next 7 dc, sl st into 1 ch.
10th round: 1 ch, 1 dc into every dc to end, sl st into 1 ch.
11th round: Using 3rd colour 1 dc into next 6 dc, 2 dc into next 2 dc, (1 dc into next 7 dc, miss 1 dc, 1 dc into next 7

dc, 2 dc into next 2 dc) 7 times, 1 dc into next 7 dc, miss 1 dc, sl st into 1 ch.
12th round: 1 ch, work in crab st in every dc, sl st into 1 ch, 16 ch, sl st into 1st ch. Fasten off.

SNOWFLAKE

Materials
1 ball (50g) Robin Columbine Crepe DK in each of 3 colours; 3mm crochet hook.
Measurements
7in(18cm) diameter.
Tension
20 tr and 10 rows to 4in(10cm).

Using 1st colour, make 3 ch and sl st in 1st ch to form a ring.
1st round: 5 ch, (1 tr in ring, 2 ch) 7 times, sl st in 3rd of 5 ch.
2nd round: Sl st in 2-ch sp, 3 ch, 4 tr in same sp, 1 ch, (5 tr in next sp, 1 ch) 7 times, sl st in 3rd ch.
3rd round: 3 ch, 1 tr into next tr, 2 ch, miss 1 tr, 1 tr into next 2 tr, (1ch, 1 tr into next 2 tr, 2 ch, miss 1 tr, 1 tr into next 2 tr) 7 times, 1 ch, sl st into 3rd ch.
4th round: Sl st in next tr and 2-ch sp, 3 ch, 1 tr 2 ch 2 tr into same sp, (3 ch, 1 dc into 1-ch sp, 3 ch, 2 tr 2 ch 2 tr into 2-ch sp) 7 times, 3 ch, 1 dc into next sp, 3 ch, sl st into 3rd ch.
5th and 6th rounds: Sl st in next tr and 2-ch sp, 3 ch, 1 tr 2 ch 2 tr into same sp, (3 ch, 1 dc into next dc, 3 ch, 2 tr 2 ch 2 tr into 2-ch sp) 7 times, 3 ch, 1 dc into next dc, 3 ch, sl st into 3rd ch.
7th round: Sl st in next tr and 2-ch sp, 3 ch, 1 tr, 2 ch, 2 tr into same sp, (3 ch, 1 dc into 3-ch sp, 3 ch, 1 dc into 3-ch sp, 3 ch, 2 tr 2 ch 2 tr into 2-ch sp) 7 times, 3 ch, 1 dc into 3-ch sp, 3 ch, 1 dc into 3-ch sp, 3 ch, sl st into 3rd ch.
8th round: Sl st in next tr and 2 ch sp. Change to 2nd colour, 3 ch, 5 tr into same sp, (3 ch, 1 dc into next sp, 6 tr into next sp, 1 dc into next sp, 3 ch, 6 tr into next sp) 7 times, 3 ch, 1 dc into next sp, 6 tr into next sp, 1 dc into next sp, 3 ch, sl st into 3rd ch.
9th round: Using 3rd colour, 3 ch, 1 tr into next 5 tr, (2 ch, 1 tr into dc, 1 tr into next 6 tr, 1 tr into next dc, 2 ch, 1 tr into next 6 tr) 7 times, 2 ch, 1 tr into next dc, 1 tr into next 6 tr, 1 tr into next dc, 2 ch, sl st into 3rd ch, 16 ch, sl st into previous sl st. Fasten off. Make a ch hanger.

Starch the potholder shapes stiffly and hang in a Christmas window. Silver glitter can be sprayed on

Tops for pots

Who could resist a pot of home-made preserves presented with a pretty cover? This is a good idea for fund-raising events as well as making your store cupboard a pleasure to see!

Materials
1 ball (25g) Twilleys Twenty; 1.75mm crochet hook; 8in(20cm) square of fabric; shirring elastic.

Measurements
To fit 1 2$\frac{1}{2}$in(6cm)-diameter pot lid.

Tension
14 dc measure 1in(2.5cm)

Lace edging
Make 144 ch.

1st row: 1 dc in 2nd ch from hook, 1 dc in each ch to end, turn.

2nd row: 1 ch, * 1 dc in each of next 2 dc, miss 1 dc, 1 htr 2 ch 2 htr in next dc, miss 1 dc, 1 dc in each of next 3 dc; rep from * to end.

Join work into a circle taking care not to twist it and fasten off.

Work in rnds along other side of base ch.

1st round: Join yarn. 1 ch, *1 dc in each of next 5 ch, 4 ch, miss 3 ch, (1 dtr 2 ch 1 dtr) all in next ch, 4 ch, miss 3 ch, 1 dc in each of next 4 ch; rep from * join to 1st dc with sl st.

2nd round: 1 ch, *1 dc in each of next 4 dc, 5 ch, 1 dtr in dtr, 2 ch, (1 dtr 2 ch 1 dtr) all in 2-ch sp, 2 ch, 1 dtr in dtr, 5 ch, miss 1 dc, 1 dc in each of next 3 dc; rep from * to end, join with sl st.

3rd round: 1 ch, *1 dc in each of next 3 dc, 5 ch, (1 dtr in next dtr, 2 ch) twice, (1 dtr 2 ch 1 dtr) all in 2-ch sp, (2 ch, 1dtr in next dtr) twice, 5 ch, miss 1 dc, 1 dc in each of next 2 dc; rep from * to end, join with sl st.

4th round: 1 ch, *1 dc in each of next 2 dc, 5 ch, (1 dtr in next dtr, 2 ch) 3 times, (1 dtr 2 ch 1 dtr) all in 2-ch sp, (2 ch, 1 dtr in next dtr) 3 times, 5 ch, miss 1 dc, 1 dc in next dc; rep from * to end, join with sl st.

5th round: 1 ch, *dc in next dc, 5 ch, (dc in next dtr, 3 ch, dc in 1st of 3 ch) 7 times, dc in next dtr, 5 ch, miss 1 dc; rep from * to end, join to 1st dc with sl st. Fasten off.

Finishing
Press crochet out to full size. Cut fabric circle to inner diameter of crochet plus $\frac{1}{2}$in(1cm) all round. Turn and sew hem for casing. Thread shirring elastic through casing. Sew crochet to edges. Draw up elastic to fit pot lid. Fasten off ends of elastic.

Thread fine elastic through the casing – knot the ends loosely

Oversew crochet to fabric hem, then pull up and fasten off elastic ends

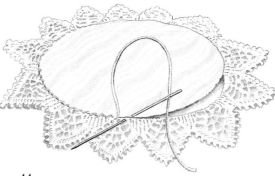

Pretty laces

Pretty laces

Crocheted edgings and insertions add a romantic touch to bedlinens, towels, tablecloths and traycloths. Attach crocheted lace as shown in the illustrations opposite.

DIAMOND DROP

Materials
1 ball (25g) Twilleys Lyscordet (makes approx. 28in(71cm) length); 2.5mm crochet hook.

Measurement
3in(7.5cm) wide.

Tension
25 sts and 13 rows to 4in(10cm) measured over trs.

Special abbreviations
cl - Cluster thus: 5 tr in next ch sp, remove hook and insert in top of 1st of these 5 tr, then in dropped lp, yrh and draw through all lps, 1 ch to complete cluster.
pct - Picot thus: 3 ch, dc in last dc worked.

Make 14 ch.
1st row: 1 tr in 6th ch from hook, 1 tr in each of next 4 ch, (1 ch, miss 1 ch, 1 tr in next ch) twice, turn.
2nd row: 5 ch, 1 tr in 1st tr, 1 ch, miss 1 ch, 1 tr in next tr, 1 tr in 1-ch sp, 1 tr in each of next 3 tr, 1 ch, miss 1 tr, 1 tr in next tr, 1 ch, 1 tr in 4th of 5 ch, turn.
3rd row: 4 ch, miss 1-ch sp, 1 tr in next tr, cl in 1-ch sp, 1 tr in next tr, 1 ch, miss next tr, 1 tr in each of next 3 tr, 1 tr in 1-ch sp, 1 tr in next tr, 1 ch, 1 tr in 4th of 5 ch, 1 ch, 1 dtr in same ch as last tr worked, turn.
4th row: 5 ch, 1 tr in top of dtr of 3rd row, 1 ch, 1 tr in next tr, 1 tr in 1-ch sp, 1 tr in each of next 3 tr, 1 ch, miss 1 tr, 1 tr in next tr, (1 ch, 1 tr in next tr) twice, 1 ch, 1 tr in 3rd of 4 ch, turn.
5th row: 4 ch, miss 1st tr, (1 tr in next tr, cl in 1-ch sp, 1 tr in next tr, 1 ch, miss 1 st) twice, 1 tr in each of next 3 tr, 1 tr in 1-ch sp, 1 tr in next tr, 1 ch, 1 tr in 4th of 5 ch, 3 ch, 1 tr in same ch as last st, turn.
6th row: Sl st along and into straight tr, 4 ch, miss 1-ch sp, 1 tr in next tr, 1 ch, miss 1 tr, 1 tr in each of next 3 tr, 1 tr in 1-ch sp, 1 tr in next tr, (1 ch, 1 tr in next tr) 3 times, 1 ch, 1 tr in 3rd of 4 ch, turn.
7th row: 4 ch, miss 1st tr, 1 tr in next tr, cl in 1-ch sp, 1 tr in next tr, 1 ch, 1 tr in next tr, 1 tr in 1-ch sp, 1 tr in each of next 3 tr, 1 ch, miss 1 tr, 1 tr in next tr, 1 ch, miss 1-ch sp, 1 dtr in next tr, turn.
8th row: 4 ch, miss 1 tr, 1 tr in next tr, 1 ch, miss 1 tr, 1 tr in each of next 3 tr, 1 tr in 1-ch sp, 1 tr in next tr, 1 ch, miss 1 cl, 1 tr in next tr, 1 ch, tr in 3rd of 4 ch, turn.
9th row: 5 ch, miss 1-ch sp, 1 tr in next tr, 1

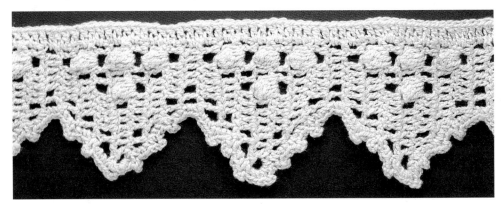

48

tr in 1-ch sp, 1 tr in each of 3 tr, 1 ch, miss 1 tr, 1 tr in next tr, 1 ch, 1 tr in next tr, turn. Rep 2nd to 9th rows for patt until length required.

Border

Work 2 dc along tr of 1st row, then *(3 dc, 1 pct) 3 times to tip of point, pct in point, 3 dc (pct, 3 dc) to lower section, 2 dc along straight trs; rep from * to end. Fasten off.

Heading

Join yarn at straight top edge. Work in tr evenly along top edge. Fasten off.

ROSE LEAF

Materials

Twilleys Twenty; 1.25mm crochet hook; narrow ribbon.

Measurement

2in(5cm) wide.

Tension

5 pattern repeats to 4in(10cm) wide.

Work ch to fit along edge, plus approximately 25cm to allow for gathers, a multiple of 8 sts plus 5.

1st row: 1 dc in 2nd ch from hook and in each rem ch to end, turn.

2nd row: 3 ch (stands as 1 tr, 1 ch), miss 1 dc, 1 tr in next dc, *1 tr in next dc, 2 ch, miss 2 dc, 1 tr in each of next 2 dc, 2 ch, miss 2 dc, 1 tr in next dc; rep from * ending 1 tr in each of last 2 dc, turn.

3rd row: 1 ch, 1 dc in each tr and ch to end, turn.

4th row: 1 ch, 1 dc in 1st dc, 2 ch, *3 ch, miss 2 dc, 1 dc in next dc, 5 ch, miss 4 dc, 1 dc in next dc, 2 ch; rep from * ending 3 ch,

miss 2 dc, 1 dc in last dc, turn.

5th row: 3 ch, *2 dtr 1 ch 2 dtr all in next 5-ch sp, 4 ch, 1 dc in next 5-ch sp, 4 ch; rep from * ending 2 dtr 1 ch 2 dtr in last lp, 1 dtr in last dc, turn.

6th row: 3 ch, *2 dtr 1 ch 2 dtr in centre of next gr, 2 ch, 1 dc in 4-ch sp, 4 ch, 1 dc in 4-ch sp, 2 ch; rep from * ending 2 dtr 1 ch 2 dtr in centre of last gr, 1 dtr in top of 3 ch, turn.

7th row: 3 ch, *2 dtr 1 ch 2 dtr in centre of next gr, 4 ch, 1 dc in centre 4-ch sp, 4 ch; rep from * ending 2 dtr 1 ch 2 dtr in centre of last gr, 1 dtr in top of 3 ch, turn.

8th and 9th rows: As 6th and 7th rows.

10th row: 1 ch, *1 dc in each of 2 dtr, 3 ch sl st to last dc for picot, 1 dc in 1-ch sp, 1 dc in each of 2 dtr, 4 dc in 4-ch sp, picot, 4 dc in 4-ch sp; rep from * ending 1 dc in each of 2 dtr, picot, 1 dc in 1-ch sp, 1 dc in each of 2 dtr, 1 dc in top of 3 ch. Fasten off.

Insert ribbon through heading, gather, allowing for extra gathers at corners.

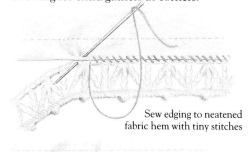

Sew edging to neatened fabric hem with tiny stitches

On an open edge, slip the needle through the fabric hem to attach edging

FLOWER SPRAYS

Materials
1 ball (25g) Twilleys Twenty; 1.25mm
crochet hook.
Measurement
Strip measures 2¹/₂in(6cm) wide.

Make 37 ch.
1st row: 1 tr in 4th ch from hook, 1 tr in
each ch to end, turn – 35 sts.
2nd row: 3 ch (stands as 1st tr), miss 1 tr, 1
tr in next tr, 1 ch, miss 1 tr, 1 tr in next tr,
(3 ch, miss 3 tr, 1 tr in next tr) twice, 2 ch,
miss 3 tr, 3 tr in next tr, 11 ch, miss 3 tr, 3 tr
in next tr, 2 ch, miss 3 tr, 1 tr in next tr, (3
ch, miss 3 tr, 1 tr in next tr) twice, 1 ch, miss
1 tr, 1 tr in next tr, 1 tr in 3rd of 3 ch, turn.
3rd row: 3 ch, 1 tr in next tr, (3 ch, 1 tr in
centre ch of next 3-ch lp) twice, 2 ch, 3 tr in
last ch before next 3- tr gr, 6 ch, 1 dc in
centre ch of 11-ch lp, 6 ch, 3 tr in 1st ch of
next 2-ch lp, 2 ch, (1 tr in centre ch of next
3-ch lp, 3 ch) twice, 1 tr in each of last 2 sts,
turn.
4th row: 3 ch, 1 tr in next tr, 1 ch, 1 tr in
centre ch of next 3-ch lp, 3 ch, 1 tr in centre
ch of next 3-ch lp, 2 ch, 3 tr in last ch before
next 3-ch gr, 6 ch, 1 dc in ch before dc, 1 dc
in dc, 1 dc in ch after dc, 6 ch, 3 tr in ch
after 3-tr gr, 2 ch, 1 tr in centre ch of next
3-ch lp, 3 ch, 1 tr in centre ch of next 3-ch
lp, 1 ch, 1 tr in each of last 2 sts, turn.
5th row: 3 ch, 1 tr in next tr, 3 ch, 1 tr in
centre ch of next 3-ch lp, 2 ch, 3 tr in last ch
before 3-tr gr, 6 ch, 1 dc before 3 dc, 1 dc in
each of 3 dc, 1 dc in ch after 3 dc, 6 ch, 3 tr
in ch after 3-tr gr, 2 ch, 1 tr in centre of
next 3-ch lp, 3 ch, 1 tr in each of

last 2 sts, turn.
6th row: 3 ch, 1 tr in next tr, 1 ch, 1 tr in
centre ch of next 3-ch lp, 2 ch, 3 tr in last ch
before 3-tr gr, 6 ch, 7 dc over 5 dc following
previous method, 6 ch, 3 tr in ch of 3-tr gr, 2
ch, 1 tr in centre ch of 3-ch lp, 1 ch, 1 tr in
each of last 2 sts, turn.
7th row: 3 ch, 1 tr in next tr, 2 ch, 3 tr in
last ch before next 3-tr gr, 6 ch, 9 dc over 7
dc, 6 ch, 3 tr in ch after 3-tr gr, 2 ch, 1 tr in
each of last 2 sts, turn.
8th row: 3 ch, 1 tr in next tr, 1 ch, 1 tr in
last ch before next 3-tr gr, 2 ch, 3 tr in ch
after 3-tr gr, 6 ch, miss 1 dc, 1 dc in each of
centre 7 dc, 6 ch, 3 tr in ch before 3-tr gr, 2
ch, 1 tr in ch after 3-tr gr, 1 ch, 1 tr in each
of last 2 sts, turn.
9th row: 3 ch, 1 tr in next tr, 3 ch, 1 tr in
last ch before 3-tr gr, 2 ch, 3 tr in ch after
3-tr gr, 6 ch, miss 1 dc, 1 dc in each of
centre 5 dc, 6 ch, 3 tr in ch before 3-tr gr, 2
ch, 1 tr in ch after 3-tr gr, 3 ch, 1 tr in each
of last 2 sts, turn.
10th row: 3 ch, 1 tr in next tr, 1 ch, 1 tr in
centre ch of next 3-ch lp, 3 ch, 1 tr in ch
before next 3-tr gr, 2 ch, 3 tr in ch after 3-tr
gr, 6 ch, miss 1 dc, 1 dc in each of centre 3
dc, 6 ch, 3 tr in ch before 3-tr gr, 2 ch, 1tr in
ch after 3-tr gr, 3 ch, 1 tr in centre ch of
next 3-ch lp, 1 ch, 1 tr in each of last 2 sts,
turn.
11th row: 3 ch, 1 tr in next tr, 3 ch, 1 tr in
2nd of next 3-ch lp, 3 ch, 1 tr in ch before
3-tr gr, 2 ch, 3 tr in ch after 3-tr gr, 6 ch, 1
dc in centre dc, 6 ch, 3 tr in ch before next
3-tr gr, 2 ch, 1 tr in ch after next 3-tr gr, 3
ch, 1 tr in centre ch of 3-ch lp, 3 ch, 1 tr in
each of last 2 sts, turn.
12th row: 3 ch, 1 tr in next tr, 1 ch, (1 tr in

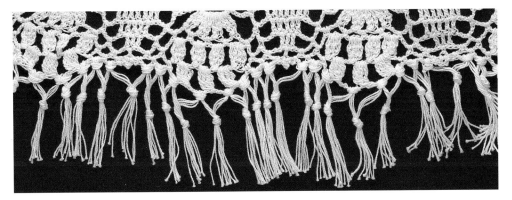

centre ch of next 3-ch lp, 3 ch) twice, 1 tr in ch before 3-tr gr, 2 ch, 3 tr in ch after 3-tr gr, 11 ch, 3 tr in ch before next 3-tr gr, 2 ch, 1 tr in ch after 3-tr grp, (3 ch, 1 tr in centre ch of next 3-ch lp) twice, 1 ch, 1 tr in each of last 2 sts, turn.

Rep 3rd to 12th rows for pattern.

Last row: Work 1 tr in each ch and tr to end. Fasten off.

SHELLS AND TASSELS

Materials:
1 ball (25g) Twilleys Twenty (to fit width of average hand-towel); 1.75mm crochet hook.

Tension:
40 sts and 20 rows to 4in(10cm) measured over pattern.

Special abbreviation
cl - **Cluster thus:** work 3 or 4 dtr as given in next lp leaving last lp of each on hook, yrh and draw through all lps.

Make a ch, a multiple of 26 sts, plus 5 ch.

1st row: Work 1 tr in 4th ch from hook, 1 tr in each of next 5 ch, *(3 ch, miss 3 ch, 1 tr in next ch) 4 times, 1 tr in each of next 10 ch; rep from * ending last rep 1 tr in each of last 6 ch, turn.

2nd row: 3 ch, miss 1 tr, 1 tr in each of next 4 tr, *(5 ch, dc in next 3-ch lp) 4 times, 5 ch, miss 1 tr, 1 tr in each of centre 9 trs; rep from * ending last rep, miss 1 tr, 1 tr in each of next 4 tr, 1 tr in top of 3 ch, turn.

3rd row: 3 ch, miss 1 tr, 1 tr in each of next 3 tr, *(5 ch, dc in next 5-ch lp) twice, 7 ch, miss next 5-ch lp, dc in next 5-ch lp, 5 ch,

dc in next 5-ch lp, 5 ch, miss 1 tr, 1 tr in each of next 7 tr; rep from * ending last rep, miss 1 tr, 1 tr in each of next 3 tr, 1 tr in top of 3 ch, turn.

4th row: 3 ch, miss 1 tr, 1 tr in each of next 2 tr, *5 ch, dc in next 5-ch lp, 5 ch, miss 5-ch lp, (3-dtr cl, 3 ch) 3 times, then 1 3-dtr cl all in same centre 7-ch lp, 5 ch, miss next 5-ch lp, dc in next 5-ch lp, 5 ch, miss 1 tr, 1 tr in each of next 5 tr; rep from * ending last rep, miss 1 tr, 1 tr in each of next 2 tr, 1 tr in top of 3 ch, turn.

5th row: 3 ch, miss 1 tr, 1 tr in next tr, *5 ch, dc in next lp, (4 ch, dc in next lp) 5 times, 5 ch, dc in next lp, 5 ch, miss 1 tr, 1 tr in each of next 3 tr; rep from * ending last rep, miss 1 tr, 1 tr in next tr, 1 tr in top of 3 ch, turn.

6th row: 4 ch (stands as 1st tr and 1 ch), *3 ch, dc in next lp, 3 ch, dc in next lp, (3 ch, 4-dtr cl in next lp) 4 times, (3 ch, dc in next lp) twice, 3 ch, 1 tr in centre of group; rep from * ending last rep, 1 tr in top of 3 ch, turn.

7th row: *2 ch, dc in next lp, (3 ch, dc in next lp) twice, 3 ch, 4-dtr cl in next lp, (5 ch, 4-dtr cl in next lp) twice, (3 ch, dc in next lp) 3 times, 2 ch, 1 dc in centre of cl top, 3 ch, sl st in last dc worked (pct made); rep from * ending last rep, 1 dc in top of 3 ch omitting pct. Fasten off.

Finishing
Cut rem yarn into 7in(18cm) lengths. Using four lengths together knot into each loop, then, taking two lengths from adjoining loops, tie four together approx 3/8in(1cm) below neatly. Trim ends to make a fringe (see detail above).

51

3: GIFTS AND BAZAARS

Little beauty

This charming little doll would make a delightful present for an adult friend. Delicately crocheted in fine cotton, the doll makes a memorable keepsake to stand on a table or a bureau.

Materials
10g Coats Anchor Mercer-Crochet Cotton No 20 in each of white, 476 (light brown), 1288/9427 (special) and 625 (light beige); short lengths of pale blue and pale pink Anchor Stranded Cotton; 1.25mm crochet hook; 24in(60cm) Offray ribbon 1/8in(3mm) wide; selection of Offray ribbon roses (or small artificial flowers); washable polyester toy filling.

Measurements
Approximately 6$^{1}/_{2}$in(16cm) high.

Tension
Diameter of head 1$^{1}/_{2}$in(4cm).

Head (back and front alike)
With light beige, make 2 ch. Mark beg of every rnd with coloured thread, moving thread up as you work.
1st row: 6 dc in 2nd ch from hook.
2nd and 3rd rows: 2 dc in each dc.
4th row: 1 dc in each dc – 24 dc.
5th row: (2 dc in next dc, 1 dc in next dc) 12 times – 36 dc.
6th row: 1 dc in each dc.
7th row: (2 dc in next dc, 1 dc in each of next 2dc) 12 times – 48 dc.
8th to 10th rows: 1 dc in each dc.
11th row: 1 dc in back lp of each of next 7 dc, 1 ch, turn.
12th and 13th row: 1 dc in each of first 7 dc, 1 ch, turn.
14th row: 1 dc in each dc. Fasten off. The last 4 rows form the neck.

Main Section (make 2)
With white, make 60 ch.
1st row: 1 dc in 2nd ch from hook, 1 dc in each ch to end, 1 ch, turn.
2nd to 12th rows: 1 dc in each dc, 1 ch, turn.
13th row: Sl st in each of first 16 dc, in back

lp of next dc work sl st 3 ch and 1 tr, 1 tr in back lp of each of next 25 dc, 2 tr in back lp of next dc, 1 ch, turn.
14th row: 1 dc in each st, 3 ch, turn.
15th row: 1 tr in 1st dc, 1 tr in each dc to last dc, 2 tr in last dc, 1 ch, turn. Rep 14th and 15th rows 11 times more, then 14th row again omitting 1 ch at end of last row. Fasten off.
Sew main sections together along underarm and side seams.

Overskirt
1st row: With rs facing, join white to first free dc lp on 12th row of main section, 1 dc in same place, *(5 ch, miss 1 dc, 1 dc in front lp of next dc) 13 times *, 5 ch, 1 dc in first free lp on 12th row of other main section; rep from * to * once, 2 ch, 1 tr in first dc.
2nd to 7th rows: 1 dc in lp just formed, *5 ch, 1 dc in next lp; rep from * ending 2 ch, 1 tr in first dc.

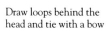

Draw loops behind the head and tie with a bow

Sew yarn loops to the top of the head

8th row: 1 dc in lp just formed, *5 ch, 1 dc in next lp; rep from * ending 5 ch, sl st in 1st dc. Fasten off.

9th row: Join special to 1st lp, 2 dc in same lp and complete as 2nd row.

10th to 19th rows: As 2nd row.

20th row: As 8th row. Do not fasten off.

21st row: 6 dc in each lp, sl st in 1st dc. Fasten off.

Sew upper sleeve seams for 1in(2.5cm) from row ends.

Cuffs

With rs facing, join Special to last row of one sleeve section, insert hook in same place and draw thread through, insert hook in next row and draw thread through, yrh and draw through all lps on hook (joint dc now made), *continuing to work over row ends (insert hook in next row and draw thread through) twice, yrh and draw through all lps on hook; rep from * ending sl st in front lp of first joint dc – 12 joint dc made.

55

2nd row: 1 dc in same place as sl st, *3 ch, 1 dc in front lp of next dc; rep from * ending 3 ch, sl st in 1st dc.

3rd row: Sl st in next ch, 1 dc in lp, *3 ch, 1 dc in next lp; rep from * ending 3 ch, sl st in 1st dc.

4th row: As 3rd row. Fasten off.

Hand

1st row: With rs facing, working behind previous 3 rows, join light beige to back lp of 3rd dc made on 1st row of cuff, 5 ch, leaving the last lp of each st on hook, work 2 ttr in same place as join and 3 ttr in back lp of next dc, yrh and draw through all lps on

hook, 1 ch.
Fasten off.
Sew open end of sleeve. Work cuff and hand to other sleeve to corrrespond.

Hat

Using white, work as head for 4 rows.
5th row: 1 dc in each dc.
6th row: As 5th row of head.
7th and 8th rows: 1 dc in each dc.
9th row: As 7th row of head.
10th to 16th rows: 1 dc in each dc.
Fasten off.

Brim

1st row: With rs facing join Special to front lp of any dc on previous row, 1 dc in same place, *3 ch, 1 dc in front lp of next dc; rep from * ending 3 ch, sl st in 1st dc.
2nd to 4th rows: Sl st in next ch, 1 dc in same lp, *3 ch, 1 dc in next lp; rep from * ending 3 ch, sl st in 1st dc. Fasten off.
5th row: Join white to 1st lp, 1 dc in same lp, *3 ch, 1 dc in next lp; rep from * ending 3 ch, sl st in 1st dc. Fasten off.

Basket

With light brown, make 4 ch.
1st row: 15 tr in 4th ch from hook, sl st in 4th of 4 ch.
2nd row: 3 ch, 1 tr in same place, *3 tr in next tr, 2 tr in next tr; rep from * ending 3 tr in next tr, sl st in 3rd of 3-ch.
3rd row: 1 dc in same place as sl st, 1 dc in each tr, sl st in back lp of 1st dc.
4th row: 3 ch, 1 tr in back lp of each dc to end, sl st in 3rd of 3 ch.
5th row: 1 dc in same place as sl st, 1 dc in each tr to end, sl st in 1st dc.
6th row: 3 ch, 1 tr in each dc to end, sl st in 3rd of 3 ch.
7th row: As 5th row.
8th row: 1 dc in same place as sl st, 1 dc in each of next 20 dc, 21 ch, remove hook from lp, miss last 19 dc made, insert hook in next dc and draw dropped lp through, miss 1 ch, 1 dc in each of the 20 ch, 1 dc in each dc, sl st in 1st dc. Fasten off. Starch all pieces and pull into shape.

Finishing

Sew head sections together leaving an

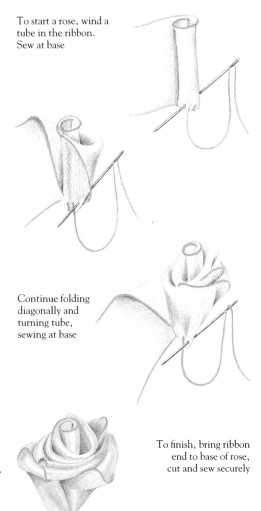

To start a rose, wind a tube in the ribbon. Sew at base

Continue folding diagonally and turning tube, sewing at base

To finish, bring ribbon end to base of rose, cut and sew securely

opening at lower neck. Stuff head and embroider eyes and mouth on front. Insert neck into upper sleeve opening and sew in position then sew up remainder of opening. Stuff main section lightly and sew opening at base. Thread ribbon through first row of overskirt, tie in a bow. Fill basket with flowers and sew to hand.

Hair using light brown, wind yarn 40 times round a 6in(15cm) piece of card, slip off loops, tie at centre, sew to centre top of head. Draw loops behind head, tie with bow in a pony tail. (See illustrations on page 54.) Decorate hat as shown in the picture on page 55 and sew to head.

Small things

This pretty, tassel-trimmed scissors case, worked in fine cotton, and glittering spectacles case make delightful gifts for a friend – but you will be tempted to keep them for yourself.

Materials

10g Coats Anchor Mercer-Crochet Cotton No. 20; 1.25mm crochet hook; 6½in(16cm) square of felt; Coats Drima thread.

Measurements

5in(12.5cm) long, excluding tassel.

Tension

First 2 rows – 1in(2.5cm) from point to point.

First side

Make 8 ch and join with sl st to form a ring.

1st round: 12 dc in ring, join sl st to back lp of 1st dc.

2nd round: 3 ch, 1 tr in same place as sl st, working in back lp only of each dc work 2 tr in each of next 5 dc, 3 ch, 2 tr in each of next 6 dc, 3 ch, sl st in 3rd of 3 ch.

3rd row: 4 ch, (1 tr in next tr, 1 ch) 10

times, 1 tr in next tr, in next sp work 3 tr 3 ch and 3 tr, 5 ch, miss 5 tr, 3 dtr in next tr, 3 ch, 3 dtr in next tr, 5 ch, in next sp work 3 tr 3 ch 3 tr, sl st in 3rd of 3 ch.

4th row: 5 ch, (1 tr in next tr, 2 ch) 10 times, 1 tr in next tr, 3 ch, 3 dc in next sp, 7 ch, 1 dc in next lp, 7 ch, in next sp work 3 dtr 3 ch and 3 dtr (shell made), 7 ch, 1 dc in next lp, 7 ch, 3 dc in next sp, 3 ch, sl st in 3rd of 5 ch.

5th row: 1 dc in same place as sl st, (3 dc in next sp, 1 dc in next tr) 11 times, 3 dc in next sp, 1 dc in each of next 3 dc, 4 dc in next lp, 7 ch, 1 dc in next lp, 7 ch, shell in 3-ch sp of next shell, 7 ch, 1 dc in next lp, 7 ch, 4 dc in next lp, 1 dc in each of next 3 dc, 3 dc in next sp, sl st in back lp of 1st dc.

6th row: 1 dc in same place as sl st, 1 dc in back lp of each dc, 4 dc in next lp, 7 ch, 1 dc in next lp, 7 ch, shell over shell, 7 ch, 1 dc in next lp, 7 ch, 4 dc in next lp, 1 dc in back lp of each dc, sl st in back lp of 1st dc.

7th to 9th rounds: 1 dc in same place as sl st, 1 dc in back lp of each dc, 4 dc in next lp, 7 ch, 1 dc in next lp, 7 ch, shell over shell, 7 ch, 1 dc in next lp, 7 ch, 4 dc in next lp, 1 dc in back lp of each dc, sl st in back lp of 1st dc.

10th row: 1 dc in same place as sl st, 1 dc in back lp of each dc, (7 dc in next lp) twice, 1 dc in each of next 3 dtr, 5 dc in next sp, 1 dc in each of next 3 dtr, (7 dc in next lp) twice, 1 dc in back lp of each dc, sl st in 1st dc.

11th round: 1 dc in same place as sl st, 1 dc in back lp of each dc to within centre dc of next 5-dc group, 3 dc in back lp of next dc, 1 dc in back lp of each dc, sl st to 1st dc.

12th round 1 dc in same place as sl st, (3 ch, miss 1 dc, 1 dc in next dc) 22 times. Fasten off.

Second side

Work as first side for 12 rows. Do not fasten off.
Next row: Place 2 sides with ws together and, working through both sides and back lps only of each dc, work 1 dc in each dc, ending with sl st in first dc on second side. Fasten off. Dampen and pin out to shape. Leave to dry.

Tassel

Wind thread 20 times around a 1¹/₂in(4cm)

piece of card. Slip off loops, tie loops ¹/₈in(3mm) from top, cut remaining loops to make tassel. Sew tassel to decorate case as shown.

Finishing

Using finished crochet as a pattern, cut two pieces of felt, sew into a lining leaving an opening to correspond with scissors case. Place lining inside, oversew to case.

SPECTACLE CASE

Materials

1 ball (25g) Twilleys Goldfingering; 3mm crochet hook; piece of red felt 7¹/₂x6¹/₄in(19x16cm).

Measurements

3¹/₂x6¹/₂in(9x16.5cm).

Tension

7 sts to 1in(2.5cm) in width.

Make 22ch.
Foundation row: 1 tr in 8th ch from hook, (2 ch, miss 2 ch, 1 tr in next ch) 8 times, turn.

1st row: 5 ch to stand for first tr and sp, (1 tr in next tr, 2 ch) 8 times, 1 tr in 5th of 8 ch, turn.

2nd row: 5 ch, (1 tr in next tr, 2 ch) 8 times, 1 tr in 3rd of 5 ch, turn.
Rep 2nd row 15 times. Fasten off.
Make another piece in the same way.

To join

Place the two pieces together, beg at top and working through both pieces, work 2 dc into each edge tr sp, each sp along chain edge and up other side.

Edging

1st round: Work 2 dc in each ch-sp all round top, sl st to beg – 36 dc.
2nd and 3rd rounds: 1 ch, 1 dc in each dc to end, sl st to 1 ch.
4th round: 3 ch, sl st to base of 3 ch (pct), *1 dc in next dc, sl st to next dc, 3 ch, sl st to same dc; rep from * all round. Fasten off.

Finishing

Fold felt in half, oversew one long, one short edge. Place inside crochet, sl st to top edge.

Bright pin-ups

Everyone needs a pincushion at some time and these delightful designs take very little time to work. Make them for gifts or for bazaars – they'll sell themselves right off the counter.

SUNFLOWER

Materials
1 ball (20g) Spectrum Dinky Detroit DK each in yellow (A) and green (B); small amount of black yarn; 3.5mm crochet hook; washable polyester toy filling.
Measurements
Approximately 6in(15.5cm) in diameter, including leaves.
Tension
20 dc to 4in(10cm).

Flower (make 2 pieces)
Using A, make 2 ch.
1st round: 6 dc in 2nd ch from hook, join with a sl st to form a ring.
2nd round: (2 dc in next dc) 6 times, sl st to 1st dc.
3rd round: (2 dc in next dc, 1 dc in next dc) 6 times, sl st to 1st dc.
4th round: (2 dc in next dc, 1 dc in each of next 2 dc) 6 times, sl st to 1st dc.
Cont to inc in this way until there are 54 dc. Work 3 rnds straight. Fasten off.

Finishing
Leaving a small opening, join the two pieces together, stuff then sew up opening.

Leaves (make 9)
Using B, make 7 ch.
1st row: 1 dc in 2nd ch from hook, 1 dc in each of 5 ch, turn.
2nd row: 1 ch, miss 1 dc, 1 dc in each dc, working last dc in 1 ch, turn.
Rep last row 4 times. Fasten off.

Finishing
Neatly sew leaves around seam on flower. Embroider eyelashes and mouth on one side as shown in picture (right).

TANGERINE

Materials
1 ball (20g) Spectrum Dinky Detroit DK orange (A), small ball green (B); 4mm crochet hook; washable polyester toy filling.
Measurements
Circumference approximately 7^{1}/$_{2}$in(19cm).
Tension
17 dc and 21 rows to 4in(10cm).

With A, make 5 ch, sl st to 1st ch form a ring.
1st round: 1 ch, 8 dc in ring, sl st to 1 ch.
2nd round: 1 ch, (1 dc in next dc, 2 dc in next dc) 4 imes, sl st to 1 ch.
3rd round: 1 ch, (1 dc in each of next 2 dc, 2 dc in next dc) 4 times, sl st to 1 ch.
4th round: 1 ch, (1 dc in each of next 3 dc, 2 dc in next dc) 4 times, sl st to 1 ch.
Work a further 4 rnds working an extra dc before the inc on each rnd – 36 dc.
9th to 11th rounds: 1 ch, 1 dc in each dc to end, sl st to 1 ch.
12th round: 1 ch, (1 dc in each of next 8 dc, miss 1 dc) 4 times, sl st to 1 ch.
13th round: 1 ch, (1 dc in each of next 7 dc, miss 1 dc) 4 times, sl st to 1 ch.
Cont to dec, as set, on next 5 rnds, at the same time stuffing as you work.
Draw up last rnd and fasten off.

Leaves (make 2)
With B, make 10 ch, miss 1 ch, in rem ch work 1 dc 1 htr 5 tr 1 htr 1 dc, 1 dc in top then along other side of ch work 1 dc 1 htr 5 tr 1 htr and 1 dc, sl st to 1 ch and fasten off.

Finishing
Sew leaves into position as shown.

Top of the morning

What fun to come down to breakfast to find your egg topped with one of these friendly little cosies! The milk jug cover is a charming, old-fashioned idea – but so practical.

EGG-COSIES

Materials
Small balls of DK yarn in colours as desired; 3mm crochet hook.

Tension
20 tr and 10 rows to 4in(10cm).

Head and body (for all shapes)
Make 4 ch and sl st in 1st ch to form a ring.
1st round: 1 ch, 8 dc into ring, sl st to 1 ch.
2nd round: 1 ch, 2 dc into each dc to end, sl st to 1 ch.
3rd to 9th rounds: 1 ch, 1 dc into each dc to end, sl st to 1 ch.
10th round: 3 ch, 2 tr into each dc to end, sl st to 3rd ch.
11th to 14th rounds: 3 ch, 1 tr into each tr to end, sl st to 3rd ch. Fasten off.

Duck's beak
Make 4 ch, miss 1 ch, 1 dc into next 3 ch, turn.
2nd row: 1 ch, 1 dc into each of next 3 dc, turn.
3rd row: Sl st into 1st dc, 1 dc in next dc, sl st into next dc.
Fasten off.
Fold in half and stitch in position.

Rabbit's ears (work 2)
Make 5 ch.
1st row: Miss 1 ch, 1 dc into each ch to end, turn.
2nd row: 1 ch, 1 dc into each dc to end.
Fasten off.

Mouse's ears (work 2)
Make 4 ch.
1st row: Miss 1 ch, 1 dc into next 3 ch, turn.
2nd row: 1 ch, 1 dc into next 3 dc, turn.
3rd row: Sl st into 1st dc, 1 dc in next dc, sl st into next dc. Fasten off. Stitch in position.

Finishing
Embroider features as shown in picture.

Larger-sized jug covers are made in the same way. Work the centre larger and add more edging

JUG SHOWER

Materials
1 ball (50g) Twilleys Secco Mercerised Cotton No 3; 3.5mm crochet hook; beads.

Measurements
9in(23cm) in diameter.

Tension
5 dc and 5 rows to 1in(2.5cm).

Make 6 ch, sl st to 1st ch to form a ring.
1st round: 1 ch, 11 dc into ring, sl st to 1 ch.
2nd round: 1 ch, 1 dc into base of 1 ch, 2 dc in each dc to end, sl st to 1 ch.
3rd round: 1 ch, 1 dc into base of 1 ch, *1 dc in next dc, 2 dc in next dc, rep from * to end, sl st to 1 ch.
4th round: 1 ch, 1 dc in each dc to end, sl st to 1 ch.
5th round: As 3rd rnd.
6th round: As 4th rnd.
7th round: *6 ch, miss 1 dc, 1 dc in next dc; rep from * to end, sl st to 1st ch.
8th round: Sl st to centre of first lp, 1 dc in same lp, *6 ch, 1 dc in next lp; rep from * ending sl st to 1st ch.
9th round: Sl st to centre of lp, 1 dc in same lp, *8 ch, 1 dc in next lp; rep from * ending sl st to 1st ch.
10th round: Sl st to centre of lp, 1 dc in same lp, *10 ch, 1 dc in next lp; rep from * ending sl st to 1st ch.
11th round: Sl st to centre of lp, 1 dc in same lp, *12 ch, 1 dc in next lp; rep from * ending sl st to 1st ch. Fasten off.

Finishing
Sew beads around edges as shown.

Cosy toes

Warm and neatly fitting these simply made slippers are ideal for relaxing in around the house – and will fold up small enough to be tucked into a weekend case. The length is easily adjusted to fit any size of foot.

Materials
2 balls (50g) Sirdar Country Style DK; 4.5mm crochet hook; ribbon for bows; chamois leather for soles (optional).

Measurements
Length of sole 9in(23cm), adjustable.

Tension
16 sts and 18 rows to 4in(10cm) in pattern with yarn used double.

Note: Yarn is used double throughout. If length of sole is adjusted make adjustment at **, then on upper work more or less dc – approx 2 dc to every 3 rows and take into account when shaping.

Sole
Beg at back of heel, make 7 ch, 1 dc in 2nd ch from hook, 1 dc in each ch to end, turn – 6 dc.
Inc 1 dc at both ends of next 3 rows – 12 dc.
Work 14 rows straight in dc. **
Inc 1 dc at both ends of next row and foll 6th row – 16 dc.
Work 9 rows straight. Dec 1 st at both ends of next 4 rows. Fasten off.

Uppers
Join yarn at centre back heel. Work 76 dc evenly around edge of sole and join with sl st to 1st st, turn.
Work 3 rows more in dc without shaping.

Shape Instep
Next row: 1 dc in each of 35 dc, dec over next 2 dc, 1 dc in each of next 2 dc, dec over next 2 dc, 1 dc in each of 35 dc, join with sl st, turn – 74 dc.
Next row: 1 dc in each of 32 dc, (dec over next 2 dc) twice, 1 dc in each of next 2 dc, (dec over next 2 dc) twice, 1dc in each of 32 dc, join with sl st, turn.
Next row: 1 dc in each of 30 dc, (dec over next 2 dc) twice, 1 dc in each of next 2 dc, (dec over next 2 dc) twice, 1 dc in each of 30 dc, join with sl st, turn.
Next row: 1 dc in each of 27 dc, (dec over next 2 sts) 6 times, 1 dc in each of 27 dc, join with sl st, turn.
Next row: 1 dc in each of 24 dc (dec over next 2 sts) 6 times, 1 dc in each of 24 dc, join with sl st. Fasten off.

Finishing
Form ribbon into tiny bows and sew to fronts. If using leather for soles, use crocheted sole for pattern, draw the shape, cut the leather to fit, then sew to sole.

Work the slippers in a soft pastel colour and trim with lace edging

As an alternative trim, add a pompon to the fronts of the slippers, or embroider colourful flowers in lazy daisy stitch. You could also sew a crocheted lace edging round the tops.

Enchanted evenings

Smart touches

Glistening narrow ribbons are exciting for crochet because the colours are rich and dramatic and the resulting texture very satisfying. The clutch bag, tie belt and wrist band are in matching colours. The floppy neck bow is made of cotton – but you could also try the pattern in lustrous black satin ribbon.

NECK BOW

Materials
1 ball (25g) Twilleys Southern Comfort;
1.25mm crochet hook.
Tension
16 spaces to 4in(10cm) measured over pattern.
Special abbreviation
pct – picot thus : 3 ch, sl st in 1st of 3 ch.

Main section
Make 26 ch. 1 dc in 2nd ch from hook and in each ch to end, turn – 25 sts.
1st row: 3 ch, (stands as 1 tr), *2 ch, miss 2 sts, 1 tr in next st; rep from * to end, turn.
2nd row: 3 ch, (stands as 1 tr), *2 ch, 1 tr in next tr; rep from * to end.
Rep 2nd row until piece measures 24¹/₂in(61cm) long, turn.
Next row: 1 ch, 1 dc in each tr and ch to end. Fasten off.

Border
Join yarn at corner and beg along narrow end. *5 ch, miss 2 squares, dc in next st; rep from * all around edge, join with sl st in 1st st.
Next round: In each 5-ch lp, work 3 dc, pct, 3 dc. Join with sl st. Fasten off.

Knot
Make 9 ch. 1 tr in 4th ch from hook and in each ch to end, turn – 7 tr.
Next row: 3 ch, miss 1 tr, 1 tr in each tr to end, turn.
Rep last row until knot measures 3¹/₄in(8cm). Fasten off.

Finishing
Form main section into bow with ends. Sew knot around centre to secure bow shape.

RIBBON PURSE
Materials
43yds(39m) of Panda ¹/₈in(3mm)-wide double satin ribbon in colour A;
49³/₄yds(45m) in colour B; 3mm crochet hook, press fastener.
Measurements
6³/₄in(17cm) wide, 4¹/₄in(11cm) deep.

Using B make 50 ch.
1st row: Using B, 1 dc in 3rd ch from hook, (1 ch, miss 1 ch, 1 dc in next ch) 23 times, 1 ch, 3 dc in last ch, now work along other side of foundation ch (1 ch, miss 1 ch, 1 dc in next ch) 24 times, turn.
Note: Join in A and B when necessary by drawing colour to be used through lp on hook, pull colour not in use firmly and fasten off.
2nd row: Using A, 1 ch, 1 dc in 1st dc, (1 ch, 1 dc in next dc) 24 times, (1 ch, 1 dc) 3 times in centre dc of 3 dc at top, then (1 ch, 1 dc in next dc) 25 times along other side, turn.
3rd row: Using B, 1 ch, 1 dc in 1st dc, (1 ch, 1 dc in next dc) 25 times, (1 ch, 1 dc) 3 times into centre dc at top, then (1 ch, 1 dc in next dc) 26 times along other side, turn.
4th row: Using B, 1 ch, 1 dc in 1st dc, (1 ch, 1 dc in next dc) 26 times, (1 ch, 1 dc) 3 times in centre dc at top, then (1 ch, 1 dc) 27 times along other side, turn.
Work a further 2 rows A, 2 rows B, 2 rows A and 2 rows B, as set on 4th row, but working the items in brackets once more on each row

and cont to work into centre top dc as before. Fasten off all ends securely.

Finishing
Fold the straight edge over 4in(10cm) to form purse. Join A to fold on one side and working through double thickness of purse, work 1 dc 1 ch evenly along side, 3 dc in corner, 1 dc 1 ch along top edge, 3 dc in corner, then 1 ch 1 dc along other side to fold. Fasten off. Fold flap over and secure with press fastener. Using A make a tassel $1^{1}/_{2}$in(4cm) long and sew to centre of purse.

BELT

Materials
$18^{1}/_{3}$yds(20.5m) Panda $^{1}/_{8}$in(3mm)-wide double satin ribbon for 7 motifs in each half, $3^{1}/_{4}$ yds(3m) to make tie; $1^{1}/_{8}$ yd(1m) Panda 2in(50mm)-wide velvet or petersham ribbon (or soft leather of similar length and width); 3mm crochet hook.

Tension
7 motifs measure 7in(18cm) long.

1st motif
Make 6 ch, sl st to 1st ch to form a ring. Into ring work 6 ch, (1 dtr 2ch) twice, 1 dtr, 4 ch, (1 dtr 2 ch) twice, 1 dtr, 6 ch, sl st to joining sl st. Fasten off.

2nd motif
Join ribbon to 1st ch of 4-ch lp and into this lp work as for 1st motif, ending sl st to 4th ch of same lp. Fasten off. Make 5 motifs more as 2nd motif was made.
Make a second piece of 7 motifs.

Finishing
Cut wide ribbon to fit your waist comfortably, plus 2in(5cm). Turn under ends to form a point and stitch. Place crochet to rs of belt, placing the 4-ch lp of each piece to each point on belt. Spread crochet to width of belt with each motif resembling a triangle and catch in position. Thread four 28in(71cm) lengths of ribbon through each point to form tie.

If using velvet ribbon for belt, you may find it better if it is mounted onto

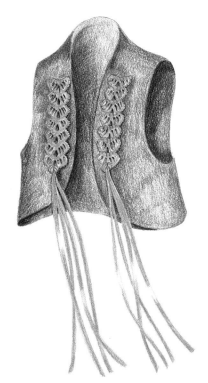

Use the pattern for the belt to make strips to go down the fronts of an evening bolero

heavyweight iron-on interfacing first, following manufacturer's instructions.

WRISTBAND

Materials
13yds(12m) Panda $^{1}/_{8}$in(3mm) double satin ribbon; 3mm crochet hook.

Measurements
Makes approximately $8^{3}/_{4}$in(22cm) of $1^{3}/_{4}$in(40mm) wide.

Make 11 ch.
1st row: (1 tr 1 ch) 4 times in 7th ch from hook, 1 tr in end ch, turn.
2nd row: 4 ch, (1 tr 1 ch) 4 times in centre sp of previous row, 1 ch, 1 tr in 3rd ch of 1st lp, turn.
Repeat to length required.

Finishing
Thread ribbons through ends and secure. Tie to fasten.

Clever carry-alls

Crocheted bags are strong and expand to take more than you would expect! Choose the one with the cherry appliqué – or the handy net bag folds up neatly into a small purse.

CHERRY BAG
Materials
2 hanks Twilleys Dishcloth cotton; small amount Twilleys Galaxia 5 in cherry red and small amount of Twilleys Lyscordet in green; 3.5mm and 2.5mm crochet hooks; washable polyester toy filling.
Measurements
12in x 14in(30cm x 35cm).
Tension
19 tr and 9 rows to 4in(10cm).

Make 63 ch using 3.5mm hook.
1st row: 1 tr into 3rd ch from hook, 1 tr into each ch to end – 62 tr counting 3 turning ch.
2nd row: 3 ch, *(1 tr through upper of 2 horizontal lps round the stem of next tr from front of work) 3 times, (1 tr through upper of 2 horizontal lps round the stem of next tr from back of work) 3 times; rep from * ending 1 tr in 3rd of 3 ch, turn.
3rd row: 3 ch, *(1 tr through upper of 2 horizontal lps round the stem of next tr from back of work) 3 times (1 tr through upper of 2 horizontal lps round the stem of next tr from front of work) 3 times; rep from * ending 1 tr in 3rd of 3 ch, turn.
Rep the last two rows until work measures 14in(35cm) from beg.
Next row: 1 ch, 1 dc into each tr to end. Fasten off. Work second piece to match. Join side and lower edges.

Handles (make 2)
Make 54 ch using 3.5mm hook.
1st row: 1 dc into 2nd ch from hook, 1 dc into each ch to end, turn.
2nd row: 3 ch, 1 tr into each dc to end, turn.
3rd row: 1 ch, 1 dc into each tr to end. Fasten off.
Stitch handles in position.

Cherries
Using Galaxia 5 and 2.5mm hook make 5 ch and sl st into 1st ch to form a ring.
1st round: 1 ch, 10 dc into ring, sl st into ch.
2nd round: 1 ch, *1 dc into next dc, 2 dc into next dc; rep from * to end, sl st into ch.
3rd round: 1 ch, 1 dc into each dc to end, sl st into ch.
4th round: 1 ch, *1 dc into each of next 2 dc, 2 dc into next dc; rep from * to end, sl st into ch.
5th to 8th rounds: 1 ch, *1 dc into each dc to end, sl st into ch.
9th and 10 rounds: 1 ch, *1 dc into each of next 2 dc, miss 1 dc; rep from * to end, sl st into ch.
Stuff centre of cherry.
11th round: 1 ch *1 dc into next dc, miss 1 dc; rep from * to end, sl st into ch.
Fasten off.

Leaves (make 4)
Using Lyscordet and 2.5mm hook make 13 ch loosely and work as follows: 1 sl st into 2nd ch from hook, 1 dc into next ch, 1 htr into each of next 2 ch, 1 tr into each of next 3 ch, 1 htr into each of next 2 ch, 1 dc into next ch, 1 sl st into next ch. Work along other side of ch as follows: 1 sl st 1 dc 2 htr 3 tr 2 htr 2 dc, 1 sl st. Fasten off.

Stems (make 2)
Using Lyscordet and 2.5mm hook make 24 ch.
Fasten off.
Stitch a cherry to each end of the stem. Stitch leaves and cherries onto bag.

The pattern could be worked in bright, two-colour stripes, omitting the cherries. Just the thing to take on holiday.

DRAWSTRING BAG

Materials
2 balls (50g) Twilley's Stalite Perlespun No. 3; 3.50mm crochet hook; washable polyester filling.

Measurements
Approximately 8in(20cm) deep.

Tensions
24 tr and 10 rows to 4in(10cm).

Make 6 ch and sl st into 1st st to form a ring.

1st round: 3 ch, 12 tr into ring, sl st into 3rd ch.

2nd round: 3 ch, 2 tr into each tr to end, sl st into 3rd ch.

3rd round: 3 ch, *1 tr into next tr, 2 tr into next tr; rep from * to end, sl st into 3rd ch.

4th and 5th rounds: As 3rd round.
Fasten off.

Work a second piece to match but do not fasten off. Place the two pieces tog and work through the two pieces as follows: 1 dc into sl st, (7 ch, miss 2 tr, 1 dc into next tr) 18 times, then working on one piece only to end, 7 ch, sl st into 1st dc.

7th round: Sl st to centre of lp, 1 dc into same lp *9 ch, 1 dc into next lp; rep from * to last lp, 9 ch, sl st into 1st dc.

8th round: Sl st to centre of lp, 1 dc into same lp, *11 ch 1 dc into next lp; rep from * to last lp, 11 ch, sl st into 1st dc.
Rep last round 15 times more.

24th round: Sl st to centre of lp, 1 dc into same lp, *5 ch, 1 dc into next lp; rep from * to last lp, 5 ch, sl st into 1st dc.

25th round: 1 ch, (5 dc into next lp, 1 dc into next dc) 5 times, *make 44 ch, miss 3 lps, 1 dc into next dc, turn 1 ch, 1 dc into next 44 ch, sl st into next dc, turn 1 ch, 1 dc into next 44 dc*, (5 dc into next lp, 1 dc into next dc) 10 times, rep from * to *, (5 dc into next lp, 1dc into next dc) to end.
Fasten off.

Button
Make 4 ch. Sl st into 1st ch to form a ring.

1st round: 1 ch, 10 dc into ring.

2nd to 4th rounds: 1 ch, 1 dc into each dc to end, sl st into 1 ch.
Fasten off.
Stuff and draw up tightly.

Button loop
Make 7 ch and stitch in position.
Sew on button.

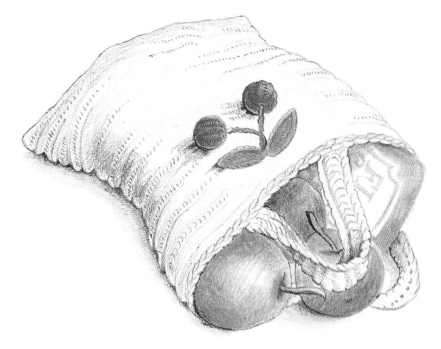

Edges in lace

Any one of these delicate crocheted laces will make a simple handkerchief a gift to be treasured. Use tiny oversewing stitches and very fine thread when attaching lace: begin and end in the middle of a side. The edgings can also be used to trim traycloths, bed linen, or even baby clothes. The edgings would also look pretty in pastel colours.

Materials
Twilleys Twenty; 1.25mm crochet hook.
Special abbreviations
cl – **Cluster** (refer to page 32).
pct – **Picot thus** : 3 ch, sl st in 1st of 3 ch.

Rosebud
Make ch to fit edge, a multiple of 6 ch plus 1.
Patt row: *Miss 2 ch, (3 tr 1 ch pct 1 ch 3 tr) all in next ch, miss 2 ch, dc in next ch; rep from * to end. Rep patt row for length required. Fasten off.

Snowflake
Beg at narrow end. Make 6 ch.
1st row: Work (1 tr 2 ch 2 tr 2 ch 1 tr) all in 6th ch from hook, 3 ch, turn.
2nd row: Work (1 tr 2 ch 1 tr 2 ch 1 tr) all in centre tr of previous row, 5 ch, turn.
Rep 2nd row for patt until strip is required length, do not turn.
Heading: *1 dc in next 5-ch lp, 5 ch; rep from * ending 1 tr in 1st st. Fasten off.

Shell
Beg at narrow end. Make 6 ch.
1st row: In 4th ch from hook make cl thus: leaving last lp on hook, work tr in each of 4th, 5th and 6th ch, yrh and draw through lps, 5 ch, 1 tr in 5th ch from hook, (2 ch, 1 tr in same ch) 4 times, 1 ttr in same place as last tr of cl was made, 7 ch turn.
2nd row: Miss 1st tr, 1 dc in next tr, 3 ch, turn.
3rd row: Leaving last lp of each on hook, 1 tr in each of 1st 3 of 7 turning ch, yrh and draw through lps, 5 ch, 1 tr in 5th ch from hook, (2 ch, 1 tr in same ch) 4 times, 1 ttr in same place as last tr of cl was made, 7 ch,

turn. Rep 2nd and 3rd rows for patt length as desired. Fasten off.

Starlight
Make ch to fit edge, a multiple of 8 ch plus 10.

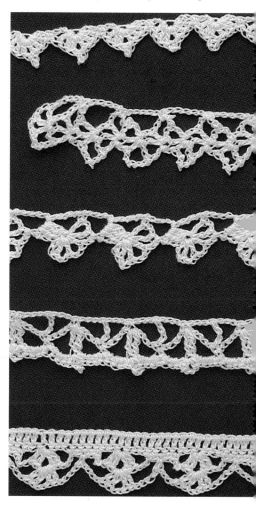

1st row: 1 dc in 14th ch from hook, *4 ch, miss 3 ch, 1 dtr in next ch, 4 ch, miss 3 ch, 1 dc in next ch; rep from * ending dtr in last ch, 1 ch, turn.
2nd row: *dc in dtr, 3 ch, leaving last lp on hook work 2 dtr in dc, yrh and draw through lps, 3 ch; rep from * ending dc in 5th of turning ch, turn.
3rd row: 1 ch, * 3 dc in 3-ch lp, dc in dtr cl, pct, 3 dc in 3-ch lp, 1 dc in dc; rep from * to end. Fasten off.

Hem the lace to the edges of a fine lawn handkerchief for a luxurious gift

Fan

Make ch to fit edge, a multiple of 10 ch plus 3.
1st row: 1 tr in 4th ch from hook, 1 tr in each rem ch to end, turn.
2nd row: 1 ch, *1 dc in each of next 3 tr, 3 ch, miss 2 tr, in next tr work (2 tr, 2 ch, 2 tr), 3 ch, miss 2 tr, 1 dc in each of next 2 tr; rep from * ending 1 dc in each of last 3 tr, turn.
3rd row: *4 ch, (2 tr 2 ch 2 tr) all in 2-ch sp, 4 ch, 1 dc in centre dc of next group; rep from *, ending 1 dc in last dc. Fasten off.

4: FESTIVITIES

Know your place

Make your Christmas table truly memorable with these jolly Santa place markers which add a festive feeling just by being there. Simply write names on small rectangles of card and stand them in front of Santa. There's also an idea for a beautiful Christmas ring.

Materials (for 3 place markers)

Coats Anchor Mercer-Crochet cotton No. 20 20g geranium (A) and 10g each light beige (B), black (C) and white (D); 1.25mm crochet hook; small beads (for eyes); washable polyester toy filling; small piece of card (for base).

Measurement

Approximately 5¼in(13cm) high.

Tension

First 3 rows of body measures 1in(2.5cm).

Main Section

Using A, make 52 ch, sl st to beg to form a ring.
1st round: 3 ch, 1 tr in each ch, sl st to 3rd of 3 ch.
2nd round: 2 ch, 1 tr in next tr, *1 tr in each of next 11 tr, leaving last lp of each on hook work 1 tr in each of next 2 tr, thread over and draw through all lps on hook (a joint tr is made); rep from * omitting a joint tr at end of last rep, sl st to 1st tr.
3rd round: 3 ch, 1 tr in each st, sl st to 3rd of 3 ch.
4th round: As 2nd rnd having 10 tr between each joint tr – 44 sts.
5th round: As 3rd rnd.
6th round: 3 ch, 1 tr in each of next 12 tr, leaving last lp on hook work 1 tr in next tr, drop A, pick up B and draw through all lps on hook, fasten off A, 1 tr in back lp only of each of next 17 tr, leaving last lp on hook work 1 tr in back lp of next tr, drop B, pick up A and draw through all lps on hook, fasten off B, 1 tr in each of next 12 tr, sl st to 3rd of 3 ch.
7th and 8th rounds: As 6th rnd working into both lps of each st.
9th round: As 2nd rnd having 9 tr between

each joint tr – 40 sts.
10th round: As 3rd rnd.
11th round: As 2nd rnd having 8 tr between each joint tr – 36 sts.
12th round: As 3rd rnd.
13th round: As 2nd rnd having 7 tr between each joint tr – 32 sts.
Cont in this manner until there is 1 tr between each joint tr. Fasten off leaving sufficient to thread through last row. Draw up last row and secure.

Beard

1st row: With rs facing attach D to front lp of 31st tr made on 5th rnd of main section, 1 dc in same place as join, 1 dc in front lp of each of next 17 tr, 1 ch, turn.
2nd row: Insert hook in first st and draw thread through, insert hook in next st and draw thread through, thread over and draw through all lps on hook (a joint dc made at beg of row), 1 dc in each dc to within last 2 dc, a joint dc over next 2 sts, 1 ch, turn. Rep 2nd row until 4 sts rem.
9th row: A joint dc over first 2 sts, a joint dc over next 2 sts, 1 ch, turn.
10th row: A joint dc over next 2 dc. Fasten off.

Hat Band

Using D, make 38 ch, join with a sl st to form a ring.
1st round: 1 dc in same place as sl st, 1 dc in each ch, sl st to 1st dc.
2nd round: 3 ch, 4 tr in same place as sl st, remove lp from hook, insert hook in 3rd of 3 ch and draw dropped lp through (a starting popcorn st made, referred to as pc st), *1 ch, miss 1 dc, 5 tr in next dc, remove lp from hook, insert hook in first tr of 5 tr group

draw dropped lp through (a pc st made); rep from * ending with 1 ch, sl st to 1st pc st.
3rd round: 1 dc in same place as sl st, *1 dc in next sp, 1 dc in next pc st; rep from * ending with 1 dc in next sp, 1 sl st to 1st dc. Fasten off.

Pompon
Using D, make 2 ch.
1st round: 6 dc in 2nd ch from hook, sl st to 1st dc.
2nd and 3rd rounds: 2 dc in same place as sl st, 2 dc in each dc, 1 sl st to 1st dc.
4th round: 1 dc in same place as sl st, 1 dc in each dc, 1 sl st in 1st dc.
5th round: 1 dc in same place as sl st, *a joint dc over next 2 dc, 1 dc in next dc; rep from * omitting 1 dc at end of last rep, sl st to 1st dc.
Fasten off leaving sufficient to thread through last row. Stuff and draw up neatly.

Base
Using A, make 4 ch.
1st round: 11 tr in 4th ch from hook, sl st to 4th of 4 ch.

2nd round: 3 ch, 1 tr in same place as sl st, 2 tr in each tr, 1 sl st to 3rd of 3 ch.
3rd and 4th rounds: 3 ch, *2 tr in next tr, 1 tr in next tr; rep from * ending with 2 tr in next tr, sl st to 3rd of 3 ch.
Fasten off.

First foot
With rs facing attach C to front lp of 16 tr made on 4th rnd of base, 1 dc in same place as join, 1 dc in front lp of each of next 8 dc, 1 ch, turn.
2nd to 4th rows: As 2nd row of beard.
5th row: As 10th row of beard. Fasten off.

Second foot
With rs facing miss next 4 tr on 4th rnd of base, attach C to front lp of next tr, 1 dc in same place as join, complete as first foot.

Finishing
Stuff main section and sew pompon, hat band and beads for eyes in position as shown in the picture on page 77. Refer to page 22 for making pompons. Cut a small circle of card, place to ws of base then sew base neatly in position.

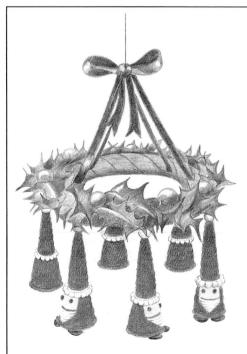

Christmas Ring
Push holly and other greenery into a florists' foam ring. Wind wide red satin ribbon over the entire ring, between the holly. Attach four narrow ribbons to the inside of the ring. Pass the ends through a brass curtain ring and knot. Tie on a large satin bow to cover the ring. Suspend the small santas, spacing them equidistantly. Glittering glass balls or other ornaments can also be added to the greenery. Thread balls on stiff wire, bend over and twist the ends, then push the wire into the foam ring. The Santa pattern is for working red dolls but they can be worked in white, green or blue to match your Christmas house decor.

Christmas boxes

*Tie these dainty little parcels to your tree for an original decoration –
they can be made in colours to match your party scheme.*

Materials (to make 3 decorations)
30 g Coats Anchor Mercer-Crochet Cotton
No. 20 main colour (M); 10g contrast colour
(C); 1.25mm crochet hook; 1¹/₈yd(1m)
Offray ribbon ¹/₈in(3mm) wide; 24 small
silver beads; foam rubber pieces cut to
2¹/₂x1¹/₂x1¹/₄in(6.5x4x3.5cm).

Measurements
2¹/₂x1¹/₂x1¹/₄in(6.5x4x3.5cm).

Tension
First 5 rows measure ¹/₈in(1cm).

Main Section
Using M, make 20 ch.
1st row: 1 dc in 2nd ch from hook, 1 dc in
each ch to end, 1 ch, turn.
2nd to 16th rows: 1 dc in each dc, 1 ch,
turn.
17th row: 1 dc in each of first 18 dc,
3 dc in next dc, 1 dc over each of next 15
row ends, 1 ch, turn.
18th row: 1 dc in each of first 35 dc,
2 dc in next dc, 1 dc over each of next 16
row ends, 1 ch, turn.
19th row: 1 dc in back lp of each dc,
1 ch, turn.
20th to 47th rows: As 2nd row.
48th row: 1 dc in each dc, turn. Fasten off.
49th row: Miss first 17 dc on previous row,

attach thread to back lp of next dc, 1 dc in
same place as join, 1 dc in back lp of each of
next 18 dc, 1 ch, turn.
50th to 65th rows: As 2nd row.
66th row: 1 dc in each dc. Fasten off.

Base
Work as main section for 1 row.
2nd to 28th rows: As 2nd row of main
section.
29th row: As 48th row of main section.

Trimming
Using C make 20 ch.
1st row: *3 tr in 4th ch from hook, 3 tr
in each of next 13 ch, sl st to first ch, 20 ch;
rep from * 3 times more omitting 20 ch at
end of last rep. Fasten off.
Make 2 lengths of 95 ch each and 2 lengths
of 75 ch each. Starch trimming, pull into
shape.

Finishing
Sew main section into box shape. Glue
paper to sides of foam pieces. Sew on
crochet. Brush lightly with starch. Fold
8in(20cm) lengths of ribbon, sew to one
corner of each box to form loops. Decorate
boxes with trimmings, beads and ribbons.

Candles for Christmas Eve

These charming candlesticks are designed with little details that make them special. They can be displayed on a shelf or table or would make unusual ornaments for place settings.

Materials (for 3 large and 3 small)

2 balls (10g) Coats Anchor Mercer-Crochet Cotton No. 20 each of 469 geranium (A), white (B), 1 ball each of 623 spring green (C), 513 orange (D); 1.25mm crochet hook; washable polyester toy filling.

Measurements

Small decoration approx 3in(7.5cm) high.
Large decoration approx 3¹/₂in(9cm) high.

Tension

First 2 rows of small decoration, ⁵/₈in(1.5cm) in diameter.

SMALL DECORATION

Base

Using B, make 4 ch.
1st row: 15 tr in 4th ch from hook, sl st to 4th of 4 ch.
2nd row: 1 dc in same place as sl st, 1 dc in each tr, sl st to back 1p of 1st dc.
3rd row: 2 dc in same place as sl st, 2 dc in back lp only of each dc, sl st to 1st dc.
4th row: 1 dc in same place as sl st, 1 dc in each dc, sl st to first dc.
5th row: 2 dc in same place as sl st, *1 dc in next dc, 2 dc in next dc; rep from * ending with 1 dc in next dc, sl st to 1st dc.
6th row: As 4th row.
7th row: 2 dc in same place as sl st, *1 dc in each of next 2 dc, 2 dc in next dc; rep from * ending with 1 dc in each of next 2 dc, sl st to 1st dc.
8th row: As 4th row.
9th row: 2 dc in same place as sl st, *1 dc in each of next 3 dc, 2 dc in next dc; rep from * ending with 1 dc in each of next 3 dc, sl st to 1st dc.
10th row: 1 dc in same place as sl st, 1 dc in each dc, 1 sl st in front lp of 1st dc.
11th row: 1 dc in same place as sl st, 1 dc in front lp only of each dc, 1 sl st to 1st dc.

12th to 14th rows: As 4th row. Fasten off

Candle

1st row: With rs facing attach A to front lp of first dc on 2nd row of base, 3 ch, 1 tr in front lp of each dc on 2nd row of base.
2nd row: 1 tr round 3 ch made on 1st row, 1 tr round bar of each tr.
3rd row: 1 tr round bar of each tr.
Rep 3rd row 13 times more, sl st to 1st tr. Fasten off.

Top

Using A, work as base for 1 row.
2nd row: 1 dc in same place as sl st, 1 dc in each tr, 1 sl st in 1st dc. Fasten off.

Flame

Using A, make 7 ch.
1st row: 1 dc in 2nd ch from hook, 1 dc in each ch. Fasten off.
2nd row: With rs facing attach D to last dc made on 1st row, 1 dc in same place as join, cont to work along other side of foundation ch, 2 dc in first ch, 1 htr in next ch, 1 tr in next ch, 3 tr in each of next 2 ch, into next ch work 3 tr and 1 dtr, 11 ch, sl st to top of last dtr (top of flame), 3 tr in each of next 3 dc, 1 tr in next dc, 1 htr in next dc, sl st to 1st dc. Fasten off.

Handle

Using B, make 25 ch.
1st row: 1 dc in 2nd ch from hook, 1 dc in each ch, 1 ch, turn.
2nd row: 1 dc in each dc, 1 ch, turn.
3rd row: Working over previous row work 1 dc in each dc on 1st row, 1 ch, turn.
4th row: Working over previous 2 rows work 1 dc in each of first 10 dc on 1st row, 2 dc in each of next 10 dc on 1st row, 1 dc in each of next 4 dc on 1st row. Fasten off.

Leaf (make 2)

Using C, make 15 ch.

1st row: 1 dtr in 5th ch from hook, 3 ch, 1 dc in top of last dtr (a picot made), (into next ch work 1 dtr and 1 tr, into next ch work 1 tr and 1 dtr, a picot) 5 times, 4 ch, in same ch as last dtr work 1 sl st 4 ch and 1 dtr, a picot, cont to work along other side of foundation ch (into next ch work 1 dtr and 1 tr, into next ch work 1 tr and 1 dtr, a picot) twice, into next ch work 1 tr and 1 dtr, miss 3 ch, sl st to next ch.
Fasten off.

Flower

Using A make 2 ch.

1st row: 5 dc in 2nd ch from hook, sl st to front lp of 1st dc. Fasten off.

2nd row: Attach B to back lp of 1st dc, 3 ch, into same place as join work 3 tr 3 ch and 1 sl st, into back lp of each dc work 1 sl st 3 ch 3 tr 3 ch and 1 sl st, 1 sl st to same place as join. Fasten off.

Make one flower using A for 1st row and D for 2nd row and one flower using D for 1st row and A for 2nd row.

Make 2 more small decorations alternating colours, as shown.

Dampen and pin out to shape.

LARGE DECORATION

Base

Work as base of small decoration for 1 row.

2nd row: 1 dc in same place as sl st, 1 dc in each tr, sl st to 1st dc.

3rd row: 2 dc in same place as sl st, 2 dc in each dc, sl st to 1st dc.

4th row: 1 dc in same place as sl st, 1 dc in each dc, sl st in back lp of 1st dc.

5th row: 2 dc in same place as sl st, *working into back lp only of each dc work 1 dc in next dc, 2 dc in next dc; rep from * ending with 1 dc in next dc, 1 sl st to 1st dc.

6th to 9th rows: As 6th to 9th rows of base of small decoration.

10th row: 1 dc in same place as sl st, 1 dc in each dc, 1 sl st in 1st dc.

11th row: 2 dc in same place as sl st, *1 dc in each of next 4 dc, 2 dc in next dc; rep from * ending with 1 dc in each of next 4 dc, sl st to 1st dc.

12th and 13th rows: As 10th row.

14th to 18th rows: As 10th to 14th row of base of small decoration. Fasten off.

Candle

1st row: With rs facing attach A to front lp of first dc on 4th row of base, 3 ch, 1 tr in front lp of each ch.

2nd and 3rd rows: As 2nd and 3rd rows of candle on small decoration.

Rep 3rd row 17 times more, sl st to first tr. Fasten off.

Top

Using A, work as base for 3 rows.

4th row: As 10th row of base. Fasten off.

Flame

Using A make 10 ch.

1st row: 1 dc in 2nd ch from hook, 1 dc in each ch.
Fasten off.

2nd row: With rs facing attach D to last dc made on 1st row, 1 dc into same place as join, cont to work along other side of foundation ch, 2 dc in first ch, 1 htr in each of next 2 ch, 1 tr in each of next 2 ch, (2 dtr in next ch) 3 times, 5 dtr in next ch, 3 ch, 1 sl st into top of last dtr (top of flame), 4 dtr in next dc, (2 dtr in next dc) 3 times, 1 tr in each of next 2 dc, 1 htr in each of next 2 dc, sl st to first dc.
Fasten off.

Handle

Using B, make 30 ch and work as handle of small decoration for 3 rows.

4th row: Working over previous 2 rows work 1 dc in each of first 13 dc on 1st row, 2 dc in each of next 12 dc on 1st row, 1 dc in each of next 4 dc on 1st row. Fasten off.

Make leaves and flowers as for small decoration.

Make 2 more large decorations alternating colours as above.

Dampen and pin out to shape.

Finishing

Fill candles with stuffing, sew flames to tops, then sew tops in position. Sew flowers and leaves at the base of each candle and sew handles in position as shown.

Santa doll

A jolly little Christmas doll that looks festive in yuletide arrangements, or could be hung on a ribbon from the tree. You could also use several on a Christmas ring – see page 78.

Materials
1 ball (20g) Coats Chain Mercer-Crochet Cotton No. 20 each of 469 geranium (A), 625 light beige (B), white (C), black (D); 1.25mm crochet hook; washable polyester toy filling.

Measurements
5½in(14cm) high.

Tension
First 5 rows of coat measure ⅝in(1.5cm).

Before commencing and using A work 2 lengths of 6 ch and leave aside for sleeves.

Coat (back and front alike)
Using C, make 28 ch.
1st row: (ws) 1 dc in 2nd ch from hook, 1 dc in each ch to end, 4 ch, turn.
2nd row: Miss first 2 dc, 5 tr in next dc, remove lp from hook, insert hook in first tr of tr gr and draw dropped lp through (popcorn st made referred to as pc st), *2 ch, miss 1 dc, a pc st in next dc; rep from * ending with 1 ch, miss 1 dc, 1 tr in last dc, 1 ch, turn.
3rd row: 1 dc in first tr, 1 dc in next 1-ch sp, 2 dc in each 2-ch sp, 1 dc in last sp, 1 dc in 3rd of 4 turning ch. Fasten off.
4th row: With rs facing attach A to first ch on other side of foundation ch, 3 ch, 1 tr in each of next 26 foundation ch, 1 ch, turn.
5th row: 1 dc in each tr, 1 dc in 3rd of 3 ch, 2 ch, turn.
6th row: Miss first dc, 1 tr in each dc to within last 2 dc, leaving last lp of each on hook work 1 tr in each of next 2 dc, thread over and draw through all lps on hook (a joint tr made), 1 ch, turn.
7th row: 1 dc in each tr, 2 ch, turn.
Rep last 2 rows 3 times more turning with 3 ch at end of last row instead of 2 ch.
14th row: Miss first dc, 1 tr in each dc, 7 ch, turn.
15th row: 1 dc in 2nd ch from hook, 1 dc in each of next 5 ch (first sleeve), 1 dc in next tr, 2 dc in next tr, 1 dc in each of next 15 tr, 2 dc in next tr, 1 dc in 3rd of 3 turning ch, attach one 6 ch length previously made, 1 dc in each of next 6 ch (2nd sleeve), 3 ch, turn.
16th row: Miss first dc, 1 tr in each of next 8 dc, 2 tr in next dc, 1 tr in each of next 13 dc, 2 tr in next dc, 1 tr in each of next 9 dc, 1 ch, turn.
17th row: 1 dc in each of first 11 tr, 2 dc in next tr, 1 dc in each of next 11 tr, 2 dc in next tr, 1 dc in each of next 11 sts, 3 ch, turn.
18th row: Miss first dc, 1 tr in each of next 12 dc, 2 tr in next dc, 1 tr in each of next 9 dc, 2 tr in next dc, 1 tr in each of next 13 dc, 1 ch, turn.
19th row: 1 dc in each of first 15 tr, 2 dc in next tr, 1 dc in each of next 7 tr, 2 dc in next tr, 1 dc in each of next 15 sts, 3 ch, turn.
20th row: Miss first dc, 1 tr in each of next 16 dc, 2 tr in next dc, 1 tr in each of next 5 dc, 2 tr in next dc, 1 tr in each of next 17 dc. Fasten off.
Sew back and front together leaving lower edge and ends of sleeves open.

Cuff
1st row: With rs facing attach C to one underarm seam and work 20 dc evenly over row ends of sleeves, 1 sl st in 1st dc.
2nd row: 3 ch, 4 tr in same place as sl st, remove lp from hook, insert hook in 3rd of 3 ch and draw dropped lp through (a starting pc st made), *2 ch, miss 1 dc, a pc st in next dc; rep from * ending with 2 ch, 1 sl st in 1st pc st.
3rd row: 2 dc in each sp, 1 sl st in 1st dc. Fasten off.
Complete other sleeve in same manner.

Front trimming
Using C, make 32 ch.
1st to 3rd rows: As 1st to 3rd row of coat.

Belt
Using D, make 47 ch.
1st row: 1 dc in 2nd ch from hook, 1 dc in each ch, 1 ch, turn.
2nd row: 1 dc in each dc. Fasten off.

Buckle
Using C, make 6 ch, 1 dtr in 5th ch from hook, 1 dtr in next ch. Fasten off.

Head (back and front alike)
Using B. make 2 ch. Mark beg of each row with a coloured thread.
1st row: 6 dc in 2nd ch from hook.

Hat
Using C, make 40 ch and, being careful not to twist ch, work 1 sl st in 1st ch.

1st row: 1 dc in same place as sl st, 1 dc in each ch, sl st in 1st dc.

2nd and 3rd rows: As 2nd and 3rd rows of cuff.

4th row: With rs facing attach A to same place as last sl st, 3 ch, 1 tr in each dc, 1 sl st in 3rd of 3 ch.

5th row: 3 ch, 1 tr in each of next 2 tr, *a joint tr over next 2 tr, 1 tr in each of next 3 sts; rep from * omitting 3 tr at end of last rep, sl st to 3rd of 3 ch.

6th row: 3 ch, 1 tr in next tr, *a joint tr over next 2 sts, 1 tr in each of next 2 sts; rep from * omitting 2 tr at end of last rep, 1 sl st in 3rd of 3 ch.

7th row: 3 ch, *a joint tr over next 2 sts, 1 tr in next st; rep from * omitting 1 tr at end of last rep, 1 sl st in 3rd of 3 ch.

8th to 10th rows: 3 ch, 1 tr in each st, 1 sl st in 3rd of 3 ch.

11th row: 2 ch, 1 tr in next st, (a joint tr over next 2 sts) 7 times, 1 sl st to 1st tr.

12th row: 1 dc in same place as sl st, 1 dc in each st, 1 sl st in 1st dc. Fasten off.

13th row: Attach C to same place as last sl st, 3 ch, a starting pc st in same place as join, 1 ch, miss 3 dc, 1 pc st in next dc, 1 ch, 1 sl st in first pc st. Fasten off.

Beard
Using C, make 28 ch.

1st row: 1 sl st in 8th ch from hook, 9 ch, 1 sl st in next ch, 10 ch, 1 sl st in next ch, 11 ch, 1 sl st in next ch, 12 ch, 1 sl st in next ch, 13 ch, 1 sl st in next ch, 14 ch, 1 sl st in next ch, (15 ch, 1 sl st in next ch) 5 times, 14 ch, 1 sl st in next ch, 13 ch, 1 sl st in next ch, 12 ch, 1 sl st in next ch, 11 ch, 1 sl st in next ch, 10 ch, 1 sl st in next ch, 9 ch, 1 sl st in next ch, 8 ch, 1 sl st in next ch, 7 ch, 1 sl st in next ch. Fasten off.
Dampen and pin all pieces out to shape.

Finishing
Thread belt through dtrs of buckle and sew front trimming and belt to coat. Sew head sections together stuffing lightly. Stuff hat lightly and sew hat and beard to head. Sew head in position to coat.

2nd and 3rd rows: 2 dc in each dc.
4th and 5th rows: 1 dc in each dc.
6th row: (2 dc in next dc, 1 dc in each of next 2 dc) 8 times – 32 dc.
7th row: (2 dc in next dc, 1 dc in each of next 3 dc) 8 times – 40 dc.
8th row: 1 dc in each dc.
9th row: 1 dc in each dc, sl st in next dc. Fasten off.

Christmas tree candles

These clever decorations are designed for the Christmas tree but they can be used in many ways – for instance as gift tags, for greetings 'cards' – or simply tape one in each window to greet your guests.

Materials (to make 3 decorations)
Coats Anchor Mercer-Crochet Cotton No. 20, 10g each of 046 geranium (A), 0759 orange (B), 0765 light French blue (C), 0131 light marine blue (D), white (E); 1.25mm crochet hook; 43in(110cm) Offray ribbon $^1/_8$in(3mm) wide.

Measurements
Approximately $5^1/_4$x$1^1/_4$in(13x3.5cm).

Flame
Using D, make 10 ch.
1st row: 1 dc in 2nd ch from hook, 1 dc in each ch to end. Fasten off.
2nd row: With rs facing attach B to first dc made on 1st row, 1 dc into same place as join, 1 htr in each of next 2 dc, 1 tr in each of next 2 dc, 2 dtr in each of next 3 dc, 5 dtr in next dc, 1 ch, cont to work along other side of foundation ch work 5 dtr in next ch, 2 dtr in each of next 3 ch, 1 tr in each of next 2 ch, 1 htr in each of next 2 ch, 1 dc in next ch, 1 ch, turn.
3rd row: 1 dc in each of first 16 sts, 3 dc in next sp, 1 dc in each of next 15 sts, insert hook into next dc and draw thread through, drop B, pick up A and draw through all lps on hook (always change colour in this way), 1 ch, turn. Fasten off B.
4th row: 1 dc in each of first 17 dc, 3 dc in next dc, 1 dc in each dc to end, 1 ch, turn.
5th row: 1 dc in each of first 18 dc, 3 dc in next dc, 1 dc in each dc to end, 1 ch, turn.
6th row: 1 dc in each of first 2 dc, (2 ch, 1 dc in next dc) 17 times, 2 ch, into same dc work 1 dc 13 ch and 1 dc, (2 ch, 2 dc in next dc) 18 times, 1 dc in next dc. Fasten off.

Candle
Using E, make 2 ch.
1st row: With rs facing work 1 dc over each of 11 row ends of flame, 3 ch, turn.

2nd row: 1 dc in 2nd ch from hook, 1 dc in next ch, 1 dc in each dc, 1 dc in each of next 2 ch, 1 ch, turn.
3rd to 11th rows: 1 dc in each dc, 1 ch, turn.
12th row: As previous row dropping E and picking up C at end of row, fasten off E, 1 ch, turn.
13th to 32nd rows: As 3rd row.
33rd row: 1 dc in each dc to end. Fasten off. Make another section in the same manner.

Joining
1st row: Place two sections, ws together, attach E to first row end of candle, working through both sections work 1 dc over first row end, 1 dc over each of next 9 row ends, 1 dc over next row end dropping E and picking up C, fasten off E, 1 dc over each row end, 3 dc in next dc, 1 dc in each dc to within last dc, 3 dc in next dc and complete other side to correspond. Fasten off.

Finishing
Dampen and pin out to shape. From the ribbon cut 8in(20cm) and thread through loop at top of flame. From remainder of ribbon cut 6in(15cm), make a bow and sew to candle.

Use the candle for a gift tag. Write a message on paper, attach with double-sided tape. Thread a gold ribbon tie through the crochet

Sweet ideas

Sugar basket

Round pieces of crochet, stiffened with sugar,
make charming baskets for table decorations or for gifts.
Handles can be made by stiffening a piece of lace insertion.
Fix handles inside basket by pinning.

Materials
2 balls (25g) Twilley Lyscordet; 2mm crochet hook.

Tension
28 sts and 10 rows to 4in(10cm) over pattern.

Special abbreviations
pct – picot: 3 ch, sl st to last of 3 ch.
cl – cluster (refer to page 32).

Beg each round with 3 ch to count as 1 tr or 4 ch to count as 1 dtr. End all rnds with sl st to 1st st. Make 6 ch. Join with sl st to form a ring.

1st round: 3 ch, 11 tr in ring.

2nd round: 3 ch, 1 tr in same place, 2 tr in each rem st to end.

3rd round: (2 tr in next tr, 1 ch, miss 1 tr) 12 times.

4th round: (1 tr in next tr, 1 tr between 2 trs, 1 tr in next tr, 1 ch) 12 times.

5th round: (1 tr in each of next 3 tr, 2 ch) 12 times.

6th round: (1 tr in next tr, 2 tr in next tr, 1 tr in next tr, 3 ch) 12 times.

7th round: (1 tr in each of next 4 tr, 5 tr in 3-ch sp, 1 tr in each of next 4 tr, leaving last lp of each st on hook work 5 tr in next 3-ch sp, yrh, draw through all lps) 6 times.

8th round: Sl st along and into 3rd tr of next gr, (1 dtr in each of next 2 tr, miss 2 sts, 5 dtr in next st, miss 2 sts, 1 dtr in each of next 2 sts, work a dtr cl joining next 2 tr cls and 2 tr of 7th rnd) 6 times.

9th round: Sl st along and into 1st dtr of gr below, (1 dtr in each of 2 dtr, 5 dtr in centre st of 5 dtr gr, 1 dtr in each of next 2 dtr, work dtr cl joining next 2 dtr, cl and 2 dtr) 6 times.

10th round: Sl st along and into 1st dtr of gr below, (1 dtr in each of next 3 sts, 6 dtr in centre st of gr, 1 dtr in each of next 3 sts, work 3 st-dtr cl over 1 dtr, cl and 1 dtr) 6 times.

11th round: Sl st along and into 1st dtr of gr below, (1 dtr in each of next 4 sts, 3 dtr in each of next 2 sts, 1 dtr in each of next 4 sts, 3-dtr cl over dtr, cl and dtr) 6 times.

12th round: Sl st along and into 1st dtr, (1 dtr in each of next 5 sts, 3 dtr in each of next 2 sts, 1 dtr in each of next 5 sts, 3-dtr cl over dtr, cl and dtr) 6 times.

13th round: *5 ch, miss 2 sts, (1 dc between 2 sts, 5 ch, miss 3 sts) 4 times, 5 ch, miss 2 sts, 1 dc on cl; rep from * 5 times.

14th round: (5 dc in each of 1st 5-ch sps, 5 tr in each of next 3 5-ch sps, 5 dc in next sp) 6 times.

15th round: Sl st along and into 3rd dc of next gr, *(4 ch, 1 tr, pct, 1 tr into centre st of 5-tr gr) 3 times, 4 ch, 1 dc, pct, 1 dc in centre dc of 5-dc gr, 3 ch, 1 dc pct, 1 dc in centre of 3-dc gr; rep from * to end. Fasten off.

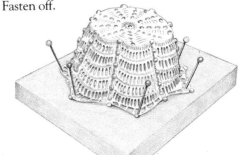

Mould the syrup-soaked crochet over an upturned bowl or dish. Pin the edges

Finishing

Dissolve 10 lumps (15ml spoons) of white sugar in quarter cup of very hot water. Soak the dish well in cooled sugar syrup. Wring out excess. Press crochet over an upturned bowl or similar shape. Pin edges, leave until almost dry then arrange points. Leave until completely dry. (See illustration, left.)

Sugar-stiffened crochet will go sticky in damp weather. It helps to spray the piece with artist's fixative or, for a permanent finish, brush with clear glue. To remove sugar, launder crochet in the usual way in lukewarm suds. Rinse carefully.

Bon-bon bags

This is a delightful idea from Europe where pretty lacy bags are made as gifts for guests on every festive occasion – weddings, christenings, birthdays and seasonal celebrations. They can be worked in any colour (think of crimson for a ruby wedding celebration) or in silver and gold. Decorate the bags with flowers, beads, ribbons or tinkling bells.

WHITE ROSES

Materials
1 ball (25g) Twilleys Twenty; 1.75mm crochet hook; small piece of net; 20in(50cm) narrow ribbon; 1 packet Offray ribbon roses (optional – or make roses from the instructions on page 57).

Measurements
5¹/₂x7¹/₂in(14x19cm).

Tension
52 sts and 20 rows to 4in(10cm) measured over filet crochet.

Front
Make 72 ch.
1st row: 1 tr in 4th ch from hook, 1 tr in each ch to end, turn – 70 sts.
Now cont in filet crochet working from the chart until 2nd – 32nd rows have been completed. Fasten off.

Back
Work as front omitting the rose motif, working in spaces and blocks as shown on chart. Fasten off.
Join sides and lower edge.

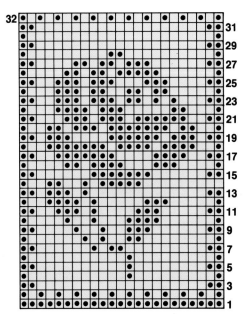

Key ◉=Block □=Space

Borders

Work evenly in dc around joined edges, having a multiple of 6 dc plus 1, turn.

Next row: *1 ch, miss 2 dc, 5 tr in next dc, miss 2 dc, 1 dc in next dc; rep from * to end. Fasten off.

Top Border

Work 1 dc in each tr and 2 dc in each 2-ch sp – 136 sts.
Cont in rounds.

1st round: *7 ch, miss 4 dc, 1 dc in next dc, 5 ch, miss 2 dc, 1 dc in next dc; rep from * to end, sl st to beg, then into 1st 2-ch lp.

2nd round: (3 ch 1 tr 2 ch) in 7-ch sp, *4 ch, 1 dc in 5-ch lp, 4 ch, (2 tr 2 ch 2 tr) in next 7-ch lp;.rep from * ending 4 ch, 1 dc in 5-ch lp, 4 ch, sl st across to 1st 2-ch lp.

3rd round: (3 ch 1 tr 2 ch 2 tr) in 2-ch lp, *(3 ch, 1 dc in next lp) twice, 3 ch, (2 tr 2 ch 2 tr) in 2-ch lp; rep from * ending (3 ch, l dc in next lp) twice, sl st across to 1st 2-ch lp.

4th round: (3 ch 1 tr 2 ch 2 tr) in 2-ch lp, *3 ch, miss next lp, 1 dc in foll lp, 3 ch, miss next lp, (2 tr 2 ch 2 tr) in 2- ch lp; rep from * ending 3 ch, sl st across to 2-ch lp.

5th round: (3 ch 1 tr 2 ch 2 tr) in 2-ch lp,

*(3 ch, 1 dc in next lp) twice, 3 ch, (2 tr 2 ch 2 tr) in 2-ch lp; rep from * ending 3 ch, sl st to 3rd of 3 ch. Fasten off.

Finishing

Line bag with net allowing a little to show at top. Sew tiny roses along lower border. Insert ribbon through 32nd row of work to tie at side with a rose to decorate.

PINK ROSES

Materials

1 ball (25g) Twilleys Twenty; 1.75mm crochet hook; small piece net; 20 in (50cm) narrow ribbon; Offray ribbon roses (optional).

Measurements

Approximately 7in(17.5cm) diameter.

Tension

52 sts and 20 rows to 4in(10cm) measured over pattern.

Make 6 ch and join with sl st to form a ring.

1st round: 3 ch to stand for 1st tr, (1 ch, 3 tr in ring) 5 times, 1 ch, 2 tr in ring, join this and foll rnds with sl st to top of 3rd of 3 ch.

2nd round: 3 ch, (2 ch, 1 tr in next tr, 2 tr in next tr, 1 tr in next tr) 5 times, 2 ch, 1 tr in next tr, 2 tr in next tr.

3rd round: 3ch, (2 ch, 1 tr in next tr, 2 tr in each of next 2 tr, 1 tr in next tr) 5 times, 2 ch, 1 tr in next tr, 2 tr in each of next 2 tr.

4th round: 3 ch, (2 ch, 1 tr in next tr, 2 tr in next tr, 1 tr in each of next 2 tr, 2 tr in next tr, 1 tr in next tr) 5 times, 2 ch, 1 tr in next tr, 2 tr in next tr, 1 tr in each of next 2 tr, 2 tr in next tr.

5th to 10th rounds: Work 6 rnds more inc 1 tr in 2nd tr each side of 2-ch sp as set. 20 trs in each of 6 sections.

11th round: Sl st to first 2-ch lp, (3 ch 1 tr 2ch 2 tr) in same lp, *3 ch, miss 3 tr, 2 tr in next tr, 3 ch, miss 1 tr, 2 tr in next tr) 3 times, 3 ch, miss 2 tr, (2 tr 3 ch 2 tr) in 2-ch lp; rep from * 5 times, ending miss 2 tr, sl st to 3rd of 3 ch.

12th round: Sl st to first 2-ch lp, (3 ch 1 tr 3 ch 2 tr) in same lp, *2 ch, 1 dc in centre of 3-ch lp, 2 ch, (2 tr 3 ch 2 tr) in 3-ch lp; rep from * ending 2 ch, 1 dc in last lp, 2 ch, sl st to 3rd of 3 ch.

13th to 17th rounds: As 12th rnd but work 1 tr instead of 1 dc.

18th round: Sl st to 3-ch lp, 3 ch, 1 tr in same lp, *2 ch, 1 tr in single tr, 2 ch, 2 tr in 3-ch lp; rep from * ending 2 ch, 1 tr in single tr, sl st to 3rd of 3 ch.

19th round: Sl st to sp between 2 tr, *7 ch, miss 1 tr, 1 dc in next tr, 7 ch, 1 dc in sp between next 2 tr; rep from * ending 4 ch, 1 tr in 1st of 7 ch.

20th round: *7 ch, 1 dc in 7-ch lp; rep from * ending 4 ch, 1 tr in 1st of 7 ch.
Rep to 20th rnd twice.
Fasten off.

Finishing
Line with net, allowing a little to show at top. Cut ribbon in half, thread through 19th rnd and tie in a bow at each side. Sew roses into position as shown.

Useful addresses

Robin Wools Ltd
Robin Mills
Idle
Bradford
W Yorks
BD10 9TE

H.G. Twilley Ltd
Roman Mills
Stamford
Lincs
PE9 1BG

Sirdar PLC
Flanshaw Lane
Alvethorpe
Wakefield
Yorks
WF2 9ND

Spectrum Yarns Ltd
Bankwell Road
Milnsbridge
Huddersfield
Yorks
HD3 4LU

Coats Leisure Crafts
Group Ltd
39 Durham Street
Glasgow
G41 1BS